SIMPLICITY

Simplicity

John Michael Talbot
with
Dan O'Neill

REDEEMER
BOOKS

Servant Publications
Ann Arbor, Michigan

Redeemer Books is an imprint of Servant Publications
especially designed to serve Catholics.

Cover design by Michael Andaloro
Title calligraphy by Susan Skarsgard

Published by Servant Publications
P.O. Box 8617
Ann Arbor, Michigan 48107

Printed in the United States of America
ISBN 0-89283-635-0

89 90 91 92 93 10 9 8 7 6 5 4 3 2 1

Contents

Preface

MY RELATIONSHIP WITH John Michael Talbot goes back to 1980 when, at the urging of a mutual friend, John called to request my assistance on a publishing project. Little did I know then what I would be getting myself into! In the beginning, John Michael asked me to write a pamphlet on his conversion to Catholicism and commitment to Franciscan spirituality in order to satisfy the many hundreds of inquiries he was receiving about his community. The pamphlet, however, quickly became a book manuscript as I began to dig into John's amazing story. This, of course, afforded me the opportunity of getting to know John Michael Talbot inside out as I read his journals, interviewed his friends, community members, his spiritual director, record industry associates, and his family. *Troubadour For The Lord* (Crossroad/Continuum, New York, New York, 1983) told the story of Talbot's personal pilgrimage and became the catalyst for numerous subsequent projects between us.

The past eight years have provided me with an excellent opportunity to observe firsthand the unfolding of John's ministry and the establishment of the Brothers and Sisters of Charity, his prayer community (also called the Little Portion) based in Eureka Springs, Arkansas. Over the years one question has continued to stand out in my mind: How is it that Talbot is able to engage his many creative projects, shoulder the responsibilities of his

Christian community, and still find time for the daily rhythms of reading and contemplative prayer?

Easy, the cynic might say. For many years he lived as a celibate monk with no wife and children. Today he still lives a married monastic lifestyle as founder and superior of the Brothers and Sisters of Charity. Isn't it easy to live the simple life when you have the support of a whole community dedicated to that purpose?

However, one visit to the Little Portion community proves this argument wrong. John could be said to have family obligations beyond most, with numerous mouths to feed, families to shelter, children to educate, property to manage and, of course, bills to pay. Not only has John founded a covenant community of single, celibate, and married brothers and sisters with its attendant legal and administrative burdens, but he also continues to write music, record albums, assist in the production of musical efforts by other contemporary Christian artists, develop book manuscripts, research the archives of church history, devour the spiritual classics, lead retreats, give lectures, perform in concerts, and travel to Third World countries in continued efforts to assist the poor through his partnership with Mercy Corps International.

How does he pull this off, I wondered, and still maintain a semblance of quiet, peace, and religious community life? Some may even suggest that such a loaded schedule runs counter to the message of simplicity which John Michael espouses.

I submit that it is precisely this commitment to simplicity which has allowed John Michael Talbot to multiply his ministry efforts in ways which have touched literally millions of lives. This is totally consistent with his philosophy of pruning. He believes in dramatically cutting back unproductive elements in our lives, ultimately allowing growth and fruit to prosper in ways that enhance spiritual development and outreach to others. Sometimes, paradoxically, less is more. That will be a concept explored in more detail in this book on simple living. In reconsidering our present lifestyles and priorities, we hope to present ways in which our lives may be more focused, simpler, and far more productive for the kingdom of God.

I will readily admit that I continue to struggle with the implementation of these concepts. In fact, I openly acknowledge my need to persist on a pilgrimage I have only recently begun in earnest. I find it a challenging and exciting adventure to live more simply, gradually embracing the sometimes elusive goal of jettisoning burdensome and unproductive baggage in order to draw closer to God and my fellow human beings. This is one of the greatest influences John Michael Talbot has had on my life. I am constantly confronted with his commitment and his practice, which I find tremendously motivating indeed.

John Michael is also inspiring many others to consider the pursuit of simplicity in a modern world of complexity, stress, technocratic values, rampant consumerism, and materialist ideals. John Michael helps us see that far from being a truly wealthy nation, we have plummeted to the very depths of spiritual poverty. He puts his finger squarely upon some of our sacred cows, creating the kind of holy discomfort which is sometimes needed to motivate us "onward and upward" in our spiritual journeys.

In the spring and late summer of 1988, I joined John Michael Talbot at his community's retreat center in giving two retreats which focused largely on simple living. It is from tapes, notes, and transcripts of these retreats that John has constructed a manuscript which beckons the serious Christian toward simplicity. John's message is not one of withdrawal from the world, avoidance of responsibility, or the shirking of burdensome worldly weights for the purpose of attaining carefree bliss. Rather, his invitation is a practical mandate urging us toward daily conversion, appropriate activism on behalf of the poor, and freedom to more fully live the gospel in our pilgrimage of faith.

Dan O'Neill

INTRODUCTION

SIMPLE LIVING SEEMS TO BE a lively topic of discussion these days, particularly in Christian circles. In fact, it's become a bit trendy to talk about getting back to the basics and giving up the fast lane for a life of quality instead of one of quantity. There is a broad spectrum of simple lifestyle philosophies which, in my experience, fall into two main camps.

The first one is more reactionary in nature. For example, as relatively wealthy Americans, we observe through the marvels of modern telecommunications the plight of the poor in Third World nations. We are struck by the desolation of a natural disaster or the withering plague of famine. We are struck with a compassionate impulse to help in some way, knowing that if we are truly Christians we should somehow make a difference. Many people will give generously during such catastrophes. Some will actually take a stab at living more simply. But for a large number, simplicity becomes a catch phrase used to pacify the conscience without making substantial, enduring life changes. There seems to be far more talk than real action many times.

On the other hand, we see more active and aggressive efforts which are based in radical—sometimes fanatical—peace and social justice ideologies. There is the attempt by some to live in destitution in order to reach the destitute. Yet very often I find that peace and social justice crusaders communicate a kind of militance and interior anger that is not healthy or godly. Among such groups there is the legitimate desire to wage war on poverty. But somehow the emphasis is on the war and on an intense kind of judgment of others which tends to eliminate any real compassion. Most average families find this kind of approach intimidating and quite undesirable.

I believe that between these two extremes there exist possibilities for authentic lifestyle changes which will not only reduce the clutter and stress we face, but will actually result in a life-giving, enriching experience for individuals, families, and groups wishing to follow the gospel of Jesus Christ in a meaningful way.

In forging a workable philosophy of simple living, it is helpful to consider the definitions of the word "simple." Webster defines "simple" as: "having only one part; being a few parts; not complicated; easy; without additions; without ornamentation; pure, unadulterated; without guile; natural or without affectation; humble, common, ordinary; unimportant; foolish or uneducated." In the Franciscan *Omnibus of Sources,* Thomas of Celano's Second Life of St. Francis of Assisi (No. 189) we find what true simplicity is. Thomas of Celano says of St. Francis:

> The saint was zealous with unusual care to show forth in himself, and he loved in others, holy simplicity the daughter of Grace, the sister of Wisdom, the mother of Justice. Not all simplicity, however, was approved by him, but only that simplicity which being content with its God considers everything else as of little value. There is that simplicity that "glories in the fear of

God . . ." This is that simplicity that examining itself, condemns no one by its judgment, that surrendering due authority to a better, seeks no authority in itself. This is that simplicity that chooses to act rather than to learn or to teach. This is that simplicity that in all the divine laws leaves wordy circumlocutions, ornaments, and embellishments, vain displays, and curiousities to those who are marked for a fall and seeks not the bark but the pit, not the shell but the kernel, not the many things but the much, the greatest and the lasting good. The most Holy Father [St. Francis] demanded this virtue in both the learned and the lay brothers, not considering it contrary to Wisdom, but true Wisdom's sister. Though he thought it easier to be gotten as a habit and more ready to be used by those who are poor as regards learning. Therefore, in the "Praises of the Virtues" he composed he says this, "Hail, Queen Wisdom, the Lord save you with your sister pure, holy Simplicity."

There's a lot in common between Webster's definition of the word "simple" and the Franciscan definition of "holy simplicity." First of all, we see that simplicity is the daughter of grace. It is a gift from God. In Franciscan theology and in scholastic theology, God was seen as the ultimate simplicity, having only one part. God also qualifies under Webster's definition of "having few parts, not complicated," as is apparent in the mystery of the Holy Trinity. Thus we see that in one God, mysteriously three persons, there is simplicity by Webster's definition. Also Francis saw the kind of knowledge which is simple and profound, not ornamented, embellished, or vain. Francis' pursuit of knowledge was therefore based in a candid, frank, and guileless approach—rejecting craftiness, cunning, and duplicity. Francis was focused on and content with God—the ultimate simplicity. He considered everything else of little value. This was the basis of his concept of gospel poverty. All else is humbled by God, all else is common by comparison, ordinary, even unimportant.

But didn't Jesus say, "...I came so that they might have life, and have it more abundantly" (Jn 10:10)? There are numerous Scriptures which are currently being used by "prosperity preachers" who would have us to believe that the sign of God's true blessing is material abundance. Many are being led to believe that if you are strong in your Christian faith, God will bless you with material abundance. After all, isn't it true that television evangelists live in mansions and drive expensive automobiles?

There is a perverted kind of teaching in churches today which unfortunately finds its way into millions of homes through the medium of television, and which elevates the created order above its original place in God's plan. Things become a sign of God's blessing. Possessions somehow authenticate true Christian faith. Of course, this goes against the essentials of Christ's teaching of gospel poverty and concern for the world's poor. It is a particular insult to Third World Christians who, in spite of their deep faith and suffering, have little to show in the way of wealth as measured by material possessions.

I believe the true approach to poverty and prosperity can be found in John 15:1-2: "I am the true vine and my

Father is the vine grower. He takes away every branch in me that does not bear fruit, and everyone that does he prunes so that it bears more fruit." Here the teachings of Jesus tell us that God desires both to cut back and to increase. He does not desire that people live in poverty, but he also does not wish that people live in an attitude of materialism and gross consumerism. In order to truly prosper in the spirit, God wishes that we prune our lives so that more fruit may be borne.

As Pope John Paul II stated in his encyclical letter, *On Social Concern* (Sollicitudo Rei Socialis, December 30, 1987), "All of us experience firsthand the sad effects of this blind submission to pure consumerism: in the first place, a crass materialism, and at the same time, a radical dissatisfaction, because one quickly learns—unless one is shielded from the flood of publicity and the ceaseless and tempting offers of products—that the more one possesses the more one wants, while deeper aspirations remain unsatisfied and perhaps even stifled" (No. 28).

It seems to me obvious that God wants to cut consumerism and materialism out of our lives. While such an approach to getting ahead would seem to be growth, it is truly an uncontrolled proliferation of materialistic pursuits which, ultimately, leads to spiritual death. Likewise, I really believe that God would like to increase material blessings for many millions of people who live in desperate poverty. God unquestionably wishes that all basic needs be met on a global basis. But the few must give up their wants in order for the many to have their needs met. Then all will be truly satisfied.

Pope John Paul goes on to state in his encyclical that,

"One of the greatest injustices in the contemporary world consists precisely of this: that the ones who possess much are relatively few, and those who possess almost nothing are many. It is the injustice of the poor distribution of the goods and services originally intended for all" (No. 28). The scandal of inequality should be obvious. Most of the world goes hungry and lives in utter poverty, while the few indulge themselves in luxury and wealth beyond all reasonable limits.

I believe, as I often repeat in my teachings, that we should live simply, so that others may simply live. It is imperative that we differentiate between our wants and our needs, because indulging our wants may actually be killing the needy. God, being loving and just, desires that all people prosper insofar as their basic human rights and needs are established, protected, and guaranteed. God desires that we live lives of quality, not quantity. I dare say that if all the peoples of the earth would live by this philosophy, the entire human family would rise to a level of well-being unprecedented in all history.

How vividly I recall a graphic example from my young adult life on a small farm in Indiana. Several rather large mulberry trees grew next to our house. Because they had grown excessively large and gangly, it was suggested that the trees be pruned. A professional crew, complete with chainsaws and hydraulic ladders, went to work. In a matter of hours a dramatic change had taken place. The previously dense fall foliage had been reduced to a few stark limbs devoid of growth. We were assured that within a year we would see the trees grow back. Sure enough, a year later a profusion of blossoming took place.

The trees grew larger, fuller, and exploded with mulberries. The pruning prescription worked perfectly.

The pruning process sometimes appears brutal. Leaves, limbs, and branches are hacked free and plummet to the ground leaving empty spaces behind. Frequently it appears as though the freshly pruned tree has been killed. It is like a radical kind of poverty—a startling simplicity which, in the end, results in fruition and abundance.

The obvious parallel is of the call to simplicity which should be taking place in our own lives. If we allow ourselves to be pruned back, much spiritual fruit will be borne in our lives. Love, joy, and peace will come forth and the gifts of the Spirit will be manifested like never before (Gal 5:22). Remember! Sometimes a pruning can be painful, but in the long run it will always be life-giving.

If we return to our Webster and Franciscan definitions of simplicity, we can see that the pruning process will involve internal and external realities. To truly understand simple living, we must begin with the internal and work outwardly towards the external. Christ, the rock of our salvation, is thrown into the pond of our lives, so to speak, sending out ripples in concentric circles. Beginning with the interior, the ripples work their way outward to our external lives and then out into the world. Therefore, the study of simplicity in our lives must begin with internal attitudes of the mind and heart so that, in the end, we may externally demonstrate the realities that lie within.

PART ONE

Inner Simplicity:
Attitudes of the Heart and Soul

ONE

Humbling Ourselves before God and Others

TRUE SIMPLE LIVING MUST begin with the heart and then ripple outward to the external dimensions of our life. It is, after all, our interior life which determines the outer realities. Put another way, our attitudes greatly influence our actions.

It is my belief that foundational to all other facets of the interior life is humility. Without humility, it is impossible to truly embark upon intentional simplicity in our lives. We see a strong indication of this in *The Rule of the Secular Franciscan Order,* approved by Pope Paul VI on June 24, 1978, the sixteenth year of his pontificate. From Section 11 of that rule, we learn:

> Trusting in the Father, Christ chose for himself and his mother a poor and humble life, even though he valued created things attentively and lovingly. Let the Secular Franciscans seek a proper spirit of detachment from temporal goods by simplifying their own material

needs. Let them be mindful that according to the gospel they are stewards of the goods received for the benefit of God's children.

Thus, in the spirit of "the Beatitudes," and as pilgrims and strangers on their way to the home of the Father, they should strive to purify their hearts from every tendency and yearning for possession and power.

This humility is further alluded to in Section 13 of the same rule, where it is stated that Secular Franciscans accept all people with a gentle and courteous spirit as gifts from God, and as Christ's image. Interestingly, the official commentary on *The Rule of the Secular Franciscan Order* begins with a section on simple living. It readily shows us the strong connection between simplicity and humility or poverty of spirit.

As the commentary reads:

Simple living also takes shape by reducing material needs, by curbing a thirst for possessions and the domineering power that comes from ownership, and by using all God's gifts in a spirit of generosity, justice, and moderation. Gospel poverty for Secular Franciscans, then, consists in acquiring possessions justly, keeping needs to a minimum, and using what they have as custodians for the generous benefit of others . . . The result of simple living and gospel poverty is freedom to seek and share the great treasure of the Kingdom: loving God and neighbor. Hand in hand with simple living is coming to recognize that in Christ all are equally brothers and sisters. There is no room for prejudice or exclusiveness in the Franciscan way of life.

In fact, the sense of commumity and the will toward community compel Secular Franciscans to discover Christ in everyone, especially the lowly and the poor and the disadvantaged.

From this we can see the connection between humility, simple living, and its many ramifications on our whole way of life.

St. Francis was humble before both the great and small alike. Because of this he had an affection for all. When he first met the powerful Pope Innocent III in the gardens of the church of St. John Lateran, the pope flippantly suggested that this ragamuffin holy man in his tattered and worn habit go roll in the mud with the pigs. Instead of being insulted, Francis willingly obeyed in abandon and joy. It was just this kind of childlike humility and obedience that won the heart of the pope for Francis. In turn, this humility opened up the whole of Europe to the Franciscans as a ripe field ready to harvest for Jesus Christ.

Likewise, Francis was humble before the humble. He always maintained it was better to obey than to be obeyed. Because of this he declared that he would obey a novice of one hour if he was appointed as his superior.

St. Clare of Assisi was enlivened by this same humility. She was known to say that even the novices of the community should be heard in chapter by the abbess, for God can work his greatest acts through the smallest and most humble of vessels.

It is just these kinds of acts of humility and obedience that caused the Franciscan movement to spread like wildfire across Europe, and eventually to the ends of the world.

TO BE BROUGHT LOW

But what does humility really mean? The word most commonly used for humble or humility in the Scriptures means to be brought low. It is literally the abasing of one's self, to be brought down, to be lower than your brother or sister and to see yourself in this lowliness. This can sometimes be a tearful, painful exercise. As has been stated by Thomas a' Kempis in his classic work *The Imitation of Christ,* "Humility can only come through humiliation." It is frequently through various levels of penance and pain that humility is achieved.

Humility is not a special gift one is born with. It *is* a gift of God. But humility is *also* acquired, so it can be learned. Remember the words of Jesus, ". . . learn from me, for I am meek and humble of heart" (Mt 11:29). In fact, Jesus frequently gave lessons on humility throughout his ministry by making such direct and powerful statements as, "For everyone who exalts himself will be humbled, but the one who humbles himself will be exalted" (Lk 14:11).

Similarly, St. Paul wrote, "Have the same regard for one another; do not be haughty but associate with the lowly; do not be wise in your own estimation" (Rom 12:16). In his letter to the Philippians he says, "Do nothing out of selfishness or out of vainglory; rather, humbly regard others as more important than yourselves, . . ." (Phil 2:3). We may therefore deduce that humility can be learned and then practiced. Paul and others tell us in the Scriptures: ". . . whatever is true, whatever is honorable, whatever is just, whatever is pure, whatever is lovely, whatever is gracious, if there is any excellence and if there is anything worthy of praise, think about these things'' (Phil 4:8). If we begin to think upon humility, to meditate upon it, we will in fact become more humble as we discipline our thoughts.

We also learn from *The Imitation of Christ* that bad habits are overcome through good habits. Remember that Paul encourages us to "associate with the lowly." Hence, we should repeatedly—even habitually—seek ways of conquering our pride through intentionally placing ourselves in the lowest place in each situation. Again, if we seek to discipline our minds by not being haughty as St. Paul urged, we will begin to discern many opportunities in everyday life to assume a posture of humility which will gradually become a way of life for us.

Remember the lesson on humility Jesus taught in Luke chapter 14:

He told a parable to those who had been invited, noticing how they were choosing the places of honor at the table. "When you are invited by someone to a wedding banquet, do not recline at table in the place of honor. A more distinguished guest than you may have been invited by him, and the host who invited both of you may approach you and say, 'Give your place to this man,' and then you would proceed with embarrassment to take the lowest place. Rather, when you are invited go and take the lowest place so that when the host comes to you he may say, 'My friend, move up to a higher position.' Then you will enjoy the esteem of your companions at the table. For everyone who exalts himself will be humbled but the one who humbles himself will be exalted." (7-11)

In this particular case, Jesus quite literally equates humility with being "brought low" in the context of a social encounter. Jesus is urging us to overcome a bad habit with the establishment of a good habit. He assists us by giving us this parable on which we might meditate, repeatedly drawing upon it for the inspiration to embrace humility day by day.

Interestingly, the above mentioned parable of Jesus also speaks to the pruning we described earlier. By choosing the lowest position at the table and cutting back on our ambition, we find ourselves winning back the esteem of our fellow guests. St. James said similarly, "Humble yourselves before the Lord and he will exalt you" (Jas 4:10). Consequently, we find that there are benefits to be realized in humility. It is only when our "branches" are cut back to truly humble levels that we will see ourselves bearing more fruit. And in seeking to be brought low, the Lord will raise us up on high.

There is an obvious danger here which must be addressed. We may find ourselves seemingly seeking humility, while harboring underlying motivations of grandeur or reward. We may seem to be humbling ourselves in attitude, when in truth, all we are really seeking is self-glorification. This, of course, is a false kind of humility. We must humble ourselves in sincerity, authentically seeking humility from the heart.

If we humble ourselves in order to be raised higher,

then we are not really humble. However, if we humble ourselves with no thought of our own advancement, then God will raise us up. It is not so much a matter of being raised up, as it is a matter of the attitude of our heart. If we are content in the lowest place then God can safely raise us up.

HUMILITY BEFORE GOD

Consider, for example, Simon Peter as he fished with discouraging results in the Sea of Galilee. Jesus urged Peter to put out again into deeper water and to lower his nets for a catch. Peter resisted, saying, "Master, we have worked hard all night and have caught nothing" (Lk 5:5). However, Peter finally agreed saying, "but at your command I will lower the nets." Of course, we know he caught an enormous number of fish which took two boats to handle. It was a great miracle which went against all logic. Peter's better judgment told him not to try again. Yet, in deference to one far greater than the greatest of fishermen, he relented only to be overwhelmed by the miraculous catch. Peter fell to his knees before Jesus saying, "Depart from me, Lord, for I am a sinful man" (Lk 5:8).

Note that there was nothing in Peter's humble response to Jesus' admonition which smacked of an ulterior motive. After all, what could Peter gain but one more tiresome, back-wrenching effort to catch what that day seemed uncatchable? Yet, because he did humble himself, he was blessed by God in a way which was totally unforeseen—even overwhelming. Peter, James, and John were genuinely awestruck to the point of fear, to which Jesus himself responded, "Do not be afraid; from now on you will be catching men" (Lk 5:10).

Peter, James, and John, because of a humble response, became party to a miracle which produced even more humility—they prostrated themselves before Christ, yielding up their possessions, choosing to follow him. This doesn't make natural sense—it certainly isn't logical when considering how to get ahead in business. It was a sincere, heartfelt humility in response to the miracle-working power of God in our lives.

We see the same kind of humble response in the story of the penitent woman in the seventh chapter of Luke's Gospel (Lk 7:36-50). Recall that Jesus was dining in the home of a certain Pharisee, when a woman known to be a sinner approached him. Her tears fell upon his feet, she wiped them with her hair, she kissed and anointed them with perfumed oil. Jesus forgave her sins. And because she was forgiven much, she loved much. The woman's act of humility became an occasion for God's mercy, extended in the forgiveness of her sins. She was brought low; she was humbled. Her humility became her opportunity for salvation. Though the woman was seeking nothing, she received everything.

Jesus' parable of the Pharisee and the tax collector in the eighteenth chapter of Luke is also of particular interest when considering the virtue of humility. Recall the words of Jesus:

Two people went up to the temple area to pray; one was a Pharisee and the other was a tax collector. The

Pharisee took up his position and spoke this prayer to himself, "Oh God, I thank you that I am not like the rest of humanity—greedy, dishonest, adulterous—or even like this tax collector. I fast twice a week, and I pay tithes on my whole income." But the tax collector stood off at a distance, and would not even raise his eyes to heaven but beat his breast and prayed, "Oh God, be merciful to me a sinner." I tell you, the latter went home justified, not the former; for everyone who exalts himself will be humbled, and the one who humbles himself will be exalted. (Lk 18:10-14)

Here again, Jesus has given another teaching on humility. Consider the individuals of the parable. The Pharisee was a member of a Jewish renewal sect which had begun some hundred years before the time of Jesus. This particular movement was a good one in its origins, and possessed zeal and devotion to the law. In fact, many early converts to Christianity were found among the Pharisees, including St. Paul, "a Pharisee, the son of Pharisees." Amazingly, many of the Pharisees believed much of what we do today, such as justification by faith and eternal life (in contrast to the Sadducees who did not believe in the life hereafter). They believed in the coming Messiah who would be born in Bethlehem. They even believed he would work miracles, be rejected by the religious leaders of his day, be put to death by them, rise again, and would ascend to heaven. The Pharisees knew from their own Scriptures that the Holy Spirit would then be poured forth on all humankind in a special way, that the division between Jew and Gentile would be broken, and that a new covenant would emerge. And it would not be based on the letter of the law, but on faith in the Messiah. Incredibly, knowing all this, they still rejected Jesus.

In studying this parable, we see that technically the Pharisee does everything correctly. He approaches with his head upraised, confident of God's mercy. He prays, giving God thanks for everything. He understands that God is the source of his salvation. Yet, in the end, he is not justified before God!

Now consider the tax collector. This man was a traitor to his people, having sold out to the Roman occupation for the purpose of making money. He was seen by his Jewish contemporaries as the scum of the earth. When he goes up to the temple he does everything wrong from a theological perspective. Instead of "boldly approaching the throne of grace," he bows, daring not to raise his eyes toward heaven. He casts himself on God's mercy, proclaiming himself the sinner that he was. He does not "claim" the legitimate gifts given the sinner by grace even under the law.

Yet the tax collector, who seemed to do everything wrong, was justified! The Pharisee, who did everything right, turned out to be wrong. Why? Because the humiliation of the tax collector was an obvious, sincere expression of failure and pain, while the arrogance of the Pharisee was quite apparent.

The humility of the tax collector is uplifted for all time in his prayer. Throughout the ages, Christian mystics have practiced the Jesus Prayer which is repeated as follows: "Lord Jesus Christ, Son of God, Saviour, have mercy on me, a sinner." This has even become a cornerstone, permanently included in the Divine Liturgy where we pray, "Lord have mercy, Christ have mercy, Lord have mercy." How far-reaching and how consequential this poor sinner's prayer was! The tax collector's exercise in humility has endured throughout the ages as the church constantly recalls his justification before the Lord.

God is interested in the attitude of the heart, regardless of punctilious attention to doctrinal detail. Before our powerful, loving God, we can only bow in submission as did Peter, as did the woman in sin, as did the tax collector.

HUMILITY BEFORE PEOPLE

Humility must apply not only to our relationship with God, but in our relationships with people. As St. Paul wrote in his letter to the Philippians, ". . . humbly regard others as more important than yourselves" (Phil 2:3). Does this mean we are to force some kind of artificial humility, disregarding our own gifts and talents? Are we to think of ourselves as being utterly no good in order to fulfill Paul's command? What about our own self-worth and identity?

Humility is simply seeing ourselves for who and what we are—no more, no less. St. Francis of Assisi said, "What a man is before God, that he is, and no more."

At this point, I feel it is important to share a major lesson in humility gained through my own life experience. In my early contemporary music career, I was riding on a wave of success which, of course, can be the occasion for pride. Then my marriage failed and I found myself face down in the dust of humiliation and emotional pain. But God seemed to give me new life—and new direction. I entered the Catholic church and experienced God's healing touch in my life. I felt complete and fulfilled as a single person and more than once publicly committed myself to a celibate life.

An interesting thing happened though: celibacy itself became an occasion for pride. While the church does not teach celibate elitism, it nevertheless exists—through human pride and weakness—in what is known as clericalism or celibate elitism. I must confess that I fell into a subtle sense of superiority and accomplishment. After some years, God again began to do a work of grace in my life which would produce a new level of humility that he knew I needed. He gave me the gift of a friendship which allowed romantic love to once again touch my life in a wholesome way.

In the midst of this friendship I ultimately had to reconsider the sacrament of matrimony. Let me stress that through the annulment of my previous marriage, it was canonically possible to marry. I would not have pursued marriage otherwise. In February of 1989 Sister Viola and I did enter into the sacrament of matrimony, transferring from the celibate-monastic expression of the Brothers and Sisters of Charity to the married-monastic expression of our community.

We did this after a year and a half of discerning God's will through the promptings of the Holy Spirit, confirmations in the Scriptures, and with discernment through both pastoral and professional counsel within the church. We did this in full compliance with the directives and norms of the Catholic church, with the full and joyful support of our community—the Brothers and Sisters of Charity—and with the almost unanimous support of all those from whom we sought counsel. After this period of discernment, I was released from my private vows of celibacy by our bishop.

In fact, our bishop presided at the ceremony, and the wedding was a joyous celebration of Jesus' love. However, this discernment was long and arduous; it was neither a quick nor an easy decision. It came through well over a year and a half of seeking God. There were even many periods of choosing to withdraw from considering the option of marriage and simply remaining in a spiritual friendship as celibates. It was from this spiritual friendship and marriage that the present community, the Brothers and Sisters of Charity, was actually birthed.

During this discernment period, I had to come face to face with my own celibate prejudice. I was a recognized celibate celebrity and to transfer into the marital state, even of a monastic community, could be misunderstood by some, even though we were supported so strongly by most. It was this confrontation with my own celibate prejudice and that of others that caused me to have to do some serious soul searching about the validity of my own celibate lifestyle. I had to come face to face with many of the weaknesses within my own soul.

As a man who had once been married, I had to confront my own fear of rejection from a failed relationship in the past. It was not so much that I was afraid to love, I was afraid to fail. In my celibacy, I thought I had confronted these issues, but now I was coming to find out that I had not confronted them fully. So I had to embrace the truth and embrace it fully without reserve.

I'm also a public figure, so this confrontation with my inner fears could not be done within my own private world. To some degree at least, it had to become public knowledge. This exposure of my private life as well as my struggles with pride regarding my celibacy caused this whole process to be a good exercise in humility.

In the end, I came to a deeper realization that I am only a human being saved by grace. I came to see that either state of life, celibate or married, should not be an occasion for pride. This is a lesson I am still learning.

I thank and praise God that the church which professes Jesus as the Way, the Truth, and the Life espouses such inner journeys when undertaken with true integrity and faith.

An important clarification is in order here. There is a difference between the wholesome interdependence I had to learn in confronting my weakness and an unhealthy co-dependence. Co-dependency is when a person who has no sense of his or her own self-worth or self-identity clutches onto another person for a sense of self-worth. This kind of relationship is mutually unhealthy. It can never set the co-dependent person free because human beings cannot save us, only God can. Likewise, it is unhealthy for the person who is being heavily relied on. It becomes a love-hate relationship. The co-dependent person will love the strong one too much and expect too much. And when the strong person manifests his or her own weaknesses and lets down the co-dependent person, the relationship will degenerate quickly into disillusionment, frustration, and sometimes even hatred.

Interdependence is an entirely different matter. This involves people who understand the truth of their own being, the truth of their dependence on God, their interdependence within the church of God, and their further interdependence with all human beings who are created in the image of God. This interdependence is based on the truth. It sets human beings free. It sets the church free. Finally, it sets all of creation free.

As we say within the guidelines of the Brothers and Sisters of Charity:

> Humility must be based on the truth . . . the truth of our own self-existence in light of the truth of God, all humankind which bears the image of God, the Church which is the temple of the Holy Spirit and the Body of Christ, and all creation which bears God's traces. It is a truth that we are dependent on God, and interdependent with the Church, the human race, and all the created world for our very self-existence. This truth of our own existence fosters both humility and a sense of positive self-worth. The humility of love cannot foster either independence or co-dependency in community. Independence denies our dependence on God, our interdependency with the Church, the human race, and the created world. It is ultimately egotistical and proud. Co-dependency seeks false dependence on God and people as a reaction to a lack of a true appreciation of self or a positive self-image. Ultimately it causes unrealistic expectations in our love relationship with

God and with people and leads to disappointment, despair, and even hate. Attitudes of independence and co-dependency work in opposition to the true charism of love, which fosters attitudes of humility based on the truth. Such an attitude of true humility is necessary in community, a mature attitude of self-love and self-worth in the Lord which breeds a positive self-image is needed by all.

Humility is simply the truth, the truth of our relationship with God and the truth of our relationship with others. And this truth is that every human being has his or her own unique gifts from God. I am incomplete if I do not recognize the uniqueness, beauty, and value of each person's gift.

St. Paul stated:

There are different kinds of spiritual gifts but the same Spirit; there are different forms of service but the same Lord; there are different workings but the same God who produces all of them in everyone. To each individual the manifestation of the Spirit is given for some benefit . . . As a body is one though it has many parts, and all the parts of the body, though many, are one body, so also Christ . . . Now the body is not a single part, but many. If a foot should say, "Because I am not a hand I do not belong to the body," it does not for this reason belong any less to the body. Or if an ear should say, "Because I am not an eye I do not belong to the body," it does not for this reason belong any less to the body. If the whole body were an eye, where would the hearing be? If the whole body were hearing, where would the sense of smell be? But as it is, God placed the parts, each one of them, in the body as he intended. If they were all one part, where would the body be? But as it is, there are many parts, yet one body. The eye cannot say to the hand, "I do not need you," nor again the head to the feet, "I do not need you." Indeed, the parts of the body that seem to be weaker are all the more necessary . . . If [one] part suffers, all the parts suffer with it; if one part is honored, all the parts share its joy. (1 Cor 12:4-7, 12, 14-22, 26)

The kind of humility of which Paul speaks is an attitude of holy interdependence within the church of Christ because the Holy Spirit has poured forth his gifts on each person as he wills. Each person, therefore, is both unique and also a common member in the whole body. This understanding should instill within us true humility before our brothers and sisters in the Lord.

Jesus extends this same concept to all of humankind in his great Sermon on the Mount where he says:

"But I say to you, love your enemies, and pray for those who persecute you, that you may be children of your heavenly Father, for he makes his sun rise on the bad and the good, and causes rain to fall on the just and the unjust. For if you love those who love you, what recompense will you have? Do not the tax collectors do the same? And if you greet your brothers only, what is unusual about that? Do not the pagans do the same? So be perfect, just as your heavenly Father is perfect." (Mt 5:44-48)

We see here that Jesus displays divine concern for all people, not just the specific people of the church.

Even the sinful human being is to be loved and respected. We are to be humbled before every human creature for the sake of God, because every human being bears the image of the God we worship. If we believe in God as Creator of the human race, we can do nothing less and nothing more. This is based on the truth of a wholesome interdependence not only between all members of the body of Christ, but among all the peoples of the earth.

In testimony to this interdependence of all of creation, St. Bonaventure echoes the theology of St. Augustine and would say that all of creation bears the traces of God. Every flower, every tree, every blade of grass, every rock, every grain of sand in some way bears traces of God. Therefore, we are to be humbled before all of creation, animate and inanimate. After all, how can we be anything but humbled when confronted with the beauty, the complexity, the overwhelming genius of God's creation? How can we be arrogant before mighty floods and raging fires? How can we be anything but humbled before ground-shaking earthquakes and the violent eruptions of volcanoes? How can we not stand awestruck at the breathtaking beauty of a green spring field decked with an array of wild flowers?

Yet amazingly we have challenged God through his creation by attempting to master it, to subdue it, and to channel it in ways which reveal our own greed and selfishness.

We have all too often failed to be wise stewards of God's creation, especially in modern times. Dangerous man-made gases daily damage the earth's precious ozone cover. Our toxic chemical waste seeps into underground water supplies. Oil spills foul waters and kill fish and birds. Acid rain destroys untold acres of forest. Even much of the processed food we eat is now so unsafe that many doctors say it may be slowly killing us! In the face of impending disaster, how can we continue to pollute our planet?

By contrast, St. Francis of Assisi could be called the greatest of ecologists—the founder of the movement itself in the true Christian sense of appreciating and seeking to nurture the goodness and glory of God's creation. The wonder of nature compelled Francis to compose the *Canticle of Brother Sun.* Here Francis displays a hierarchy of values very much in keeping with the theology of the Christian masters of antiquity, even though Francis himself was schooled in none of their writings.

First, he ascribes all praise to God, saying, "Most high, all powerful, all good, Lord! All praise is yours, all glory, all honor, and all blessing. To you, alone, most high, do they belong. No mortal lips are worthy to pronounce your name." Then he praises God for the created world in one of the most inspiring hymns ever composed:

All praise is yours, my Lord, through all that you have made, and first my Lord; brother Sun who brings the day; and light you give to us through him. How beautiful is he, how radiant in all his splendor! Of you, most high, he bears the likeness.

Francis saw more than God's traces in nature, he

observed God's likeness in nature, an eternal metaphor of divine proportions.

Francis went on to speak of sister Moon and the stars, brothers Wind and Air, sister Water, precious and pure, brother Fire, full of power and strength, and sister Earth, our mother who feeds us and produces fruits, flowers, and herbs.

Such humility before all the created world, could it be possessed by us all, would deter the arrogant exploitation of creation which threatens the existence of human beings and the destruction of the planet.

THE FRANCISCAN AND MONASTIC VIRTUE OF HUMILITY

Thomas of Celano, in his *Second Life of St. Francis* says, "Humility is the guardian and the ornament of all virtues. If the spiritual building does not rest upon it, it will fall into ruin, though it seems to be growing" (No. 140). Jesus himself begins the Beatitudes with "poverty of spirit." The definition of poverty of spirit is strongly related to the concept of humility. It refers to interior reality—to that attitude of humility and simplicity which precedes external actions. I believe this is why Jesus initiated the Beatitudes with the spiritual dimension of poverty.

Likewise, the *Rule of St. Benedict* places much importance on humility as the cornerstone of virtue. In Benedict's treatment of obedience, he begins with humility saying, "The first degree of humility is obedience without delay."

He then proceeds in chapter seven of the *Rule* to give us twelve degrees of humility.

1. Keeping the fear of God before one's eyes;
2. Loving not one's own will, delighting not in gratifying one's desires, but carrying out deeds in the spirit of the Lord, "I do not seek my own will but the will of the one who sent me" (Jn 5:30);
3. That a person for the love of God submit himself to his superior in all obedience;
4. That in this very obedience to hard and contrary things, even when injuries are done, one should take hold silently in patience and bearing up bravely, grow not weary nor depart, according to that saying in Scripture, "By your perseverance you will secure your lives" (Lk 21:19);
5. Not to conceal from one's habits the evil thoughts that beset one's heart, nor the sins committed in secret, but to manifest them in humble confession;
6. That a monk be content with all that is mean and poor and in all that is enjoined on him, esteem himself a sinful and unworthy laborer saying with the prophet, "I was stupid and understood not;/I was like a brute beast in your presence./Yet with you I shall always be" (Ps 73:22-23);
7. That a person not only call himself, with his own tongue, lower and viler than all men, but also consider himself thus within those convictions, humbling himself and saying with the prophet, ". . . I am a worm, not a man;/the scorn of men, despised by the people" (Ps 22:7);

8. That a monk do nothing except what the common rule of the monastery or the example of the seniors direct;

9. That a monk restrain his tongue from speaking and maintaining silence, speak not until questioned;

10. That one be not easily moved or quick to laughter because it is written, "The fool lifts up his head in laughter";

11. That when a monk speaks, he do so gently and without laughter, humbly, gravely, and with few and reasonable words;

12. That a monk not only in his heart, but also in his very outward appearance, always show his humility to all who see him. That is, in his oratory, in the monastery, in the garden, when traveling, in the field, or wherever he may be, whether sitting, walking, or standing, he should always keep his head bent down, his gaze fixed to the ground.

The Rule of St. Benedict, in its treatment of humility, permeates many areas of human behavior and touches on many other virtues. Of course, the rule was designed specifically for monks and doesn't equally apply to all Christian men and women. But humility is at its center. Therefore, the rule can be instructive to all Christians by helping form in us an attitude of humility. Likewise, St. Francis and subsequent Franciscan leaders followed the example of great monastic traditions and placed the virtue of humility as a cornerstone in the foundation on which they built.

I am continually drawn to the life of St. Francis of Assisi.

His life exemplified, perhaps more than any other, the virtue of humility. Among his admonitions on being a humble servant of God he states, "Blessed [is he] who takes no more pride in the good that God says and does through him, than that which he says and does through someone else." Francis could only say this because he recognized not only with his mind, but with his heart the true interdependence of the individual members of the church. When the blessings of God are poured out on one member, they are poured out on all. As Paul said, "If [one] part suffers, all the parts suffer with it. If one part is honored, all the parts share its joy" (1 Cor 12:26).

St. Francis believed that we are to recognize the authority of all our brothers and sisters in Christ, not just those who hold formal positions of authority. Therefore, the least of the brethren were to be considered superior, while the most superior were to conduct themselves as the least. Thomas of Celano wrote that Francis was, "humble in dress, more humble in conviction, most humble in reputation." Even so, Francis desired to lower himself even further by actually resigning his position as superior of the order he himself founded. In his writings, Celano tells us Francis said that:

Those who are put in charge of others should be no prouder of their office than if they had been appointed to wash the feet of their confreres. They should be no more upset by the loss of their authority than they would if they were deprived of the task of washing feet. The more they are upset, the greater risk they incur in their soul.

Francis, in fact, strongly encouraged his Franciscan brothers not to seek any office of authority whatsoever. This doesn't mean you have to convince yourself that you are the world's worst person. But it does mean you should always be ready to take the lowest position by serving others.

Seeking authority, he reasoned, or even accepting it, could result in the occasion of pride, the ultimate sin. Of course, we shouldn't flee if God calls us to leadership. Rather, we should seek God's will in all humility and submit to his direction.

We must, as the Scriptures teach, die to self and thereby die to pride. We must allow the lessons of humility to permeate our entire lives so that we might be called and not driven. If we simply let go and let God do his work of humility in our lives, arrogance will give way to true confidence in the realization of who we are before God and before others.

In the final analysis, St. Francis, like St. Paul before him, knew that sin is the great leveler of all humankind. All have sinned and fallen short of God's glory, therefore, all must be humbled by the sinless Christ. The journey toward simplicity must begin with a stark, simple realization: we are all sinners saved by God's grace, the realization of which can only produce humility. Humility, then, is the first essential interior ingredient if we are to proceed upon our pilgrimage toward true simplicity of life. Let us ask God for the precious gift of humility. And let us always seek to serve others first.

Practical Pointers for Growing in Humility:

1) Give some examples of your own legitimate gifts from

God. Do you give God the glory and credit for these gifts? Or do you claim all the credit yourself?

2) Do you recognize your interdependence with others and with all of creation? Do you ever become co-dependent upon others? Or are you making the opposite mistake by seeking to be too independent and self-reliant?

3) Name some specific areas in your life where you need to grow in humility. Develop a plan for growing in one key area over the next two weeks.

TWO

Obedience: Our Response in Love

I T'S A WORD MOST MODERN AMERICANS don't like to hear. Yet obedience is important in a complicated world and is directly related to humility. It may even be called an expression of humility. St. Francis of Assisi believed it was very important to understand that humble obedience is, in fact, an essential dimension to gospel poverty. "A man takes leave of all that he possesses and loses both his body and his life when he gives himself up completely to obedience in the hands of his superior," he said.

Let's recall the story of St. Francis from the last chapter as an example. Because Francis was willing to obey the pope, even to the point of rolling in the mud with the pigs, God raised him up as an evangelist to the whole Christian world, and even to the Moslems. This is not only a lesson in humility, it is also a powerful lesson in obedience. Obeying the pope meant lowering himself in the sight of all, but God raised him up and used him in marvelous ways.

As we have seen in the *Rule of St. Benedict,* there is strong linkage between humility and obedience to varying degrees. First, according to St. Benedict, humility is obedience without delay. Second, we must hear God's word and conform our will to his will. Third, a person should submit to superiors in all obedience, in imitation of the Lord who became obedient even unto death. Fourth, a person should endure adversity and injury in silent patience. And fifth, sin should not be held in secret but manifested in humble confession. For both St. Francis and St. Benedict, obedience is considered a direct result of humility—it is an evidence of a humble heart before God.

Our lives need to be channeled and directed, much like a river. As the banks of the river provide limits for the flow of water, so authority directs and channels the life of the church—and the individual believer. Obedience is the recognition of the "river banks" which God places in the flow of our pilgrimage through life.

The Scriptures give us much instruction in obedience. First Samuel 15:22 says, "Does the LORD so delight in holocausts and sacrifices as in obedience to the command of the LORD? Obedience is better than sacrifice," . . . We find that even in the Old Testament it was not enough to merely go through the motions of ritual sacrifice in worship of God. The sacrifice was ratified by a deeper, underlying attitude of humility and obedience to God. God was and is concerned not so much with what we do, but with the disposition of our hearts.

OBEDIENCE TO GOD

Jesus shattered the idea of mere ritual performance, placing a high degree of importance on heartfelt obedience to God. "If you love me, you will keep my commandments" (Jn 14:15), he stated unequivocally. "For whoever does the will of my heavenly Father is my brother, and sister, and mother" (Mt 12:50). In John's Gospel, Christ enjoined his listeners, "If you keep my commandments, you will remain in my love, just as I have kept my Father's commandments and remain in his love" (Jn 15:10). Jesus strongly relates obedience to love.

Obviously, then, obedience is not merely a legal injunction but a love response to God: a love response directly related to the concept of true humility before God Almighty. We are told in the New Testament that if our humility and love result in holy obedience, our holiness will actually surpass that of the scribes and Pharisees (Mt 5:20).

Obedience, however, *is not always easy.* Frequently our Christian commitment requires of us an attitude, a word, or an action which runs contrary to our natural will. It should be comforting for us to realize at this point that we are not alone in this. In fact, Jesus himself became like us to the point where he was able to sympathize with our every weakness, tempted in every way that we are. Yet he never sinned. Witness the extraordinary commitment to obedience which Jesus expressed to God the Father in the Garden of Gethsemane before his crucifixion. In his prayer, he lifted his heart in great anxiety before God saying: "Father, if you are willing, take this cup away from me; still, not my will but yours be done" (Lk 22:42). Recall that in Luke's Gospel the anxiety of Christ was so great that "He was in such agony and he prayed so fervently that sweat became like drops of blood falling on the ground" (Lk 22:44). Obedience is not always easy. It is sometimes a supreme test of faith.

In the Book of Hebrews it is written:

> Son though he was, he learned obedience from what he suffered; and when he was made perfect, he became the source of eternal salvation for all who obey him, declared by God high priest according to the order of Melchizedek. (Heb 5:8-10).

Therefore, we know that Jesus himself suffered in being obedient to the Father, so he would be able to strengthen us as we suffer and struggle in obedient service to God through times of trial, anxiety, and temptation.

These challenges, when met with humble obedience, work for the strengthening of our faith. And again, we can learn from the example of Jesus as we read in Hebrews, "For it was fitting that he, for whom and through whom all things exist, in bringing many children to glory, should make the leader to their salvation perfect through suffering" (Heb 2:10). It is, therefore, through suffering and trial that perfection is attained. As Peter says in his first epistle:

> In this you rejoice, although now for a little while you may have to suffer through serious trials, so that the

genuineness of your faith, more precious than gold that is perishable even though tested by fire, may prove to be for praise, glory, and honor at the revelation of Jesus Christ. (1 Pt 1:6-7)

When we are obedient in hard times, we are made strong. After all, Jesus never escaped them. His ministry began with temptation in the desert and ended with agony in Gethsemane and death upon the cross. But through obedience his resurrection conquered sin and death.

OBEDIENCE TO GOD IS OBEDIENCE TO OTHERS

It is not enough to simply be obedient to God alone. We must maintain an attitude of obedience to others and even to the laws of creation. We should express a humble obedience toward the laws of creation because they bear the imprint of the Creator; we should be humbly obedient to all human beings since they bear the image of God within their soul. We are obedient to the church because it is the body of Christ. As was the case with humility, we find that obedience also becomes an expression of interdependence.

We are beginning to see, in this generation as never before, what the consequences can be of disobedience to the created world. When we attempt to circumvent the natural cycles of nature through our technology, catastrophe can result. The consequences of unbridled slash-and-burn agricultural techniques in the Third World, for example, are now becoming apparent. Many scientists say that such destruction of forests in the Amazon is actually beginning to affect weather cycles on an international basis. Failure to flee before the destructive power of hurricanes has resulted in death and injury. In all our scientific genius, we cower in fear before the seismic horrors of earthquakes.

We also find ourselves mandated by God himself to be obedient to civil forms of government. Government, we are told in Scripture, has been instituted by none other than God himself. When functioning as God intended it, civil law protects the innocent, encourages order in society, and restrains evil through legal sanctions (Rom 13:1-7).

Of course, in using the examples of obedience to civil authority in Scripture, we must keep in mind the historical circumstances of the Roman occupation of Israel. Since the first Christians had virtually no voice in that government, an almost resigned obedience was the most positive way to prove their intentions of peace. Later in history, after Constantine openly welcomed Christianity into the Roman Empire, a more active participation in government by Christians became possible. This is illustrated by the stern words of St. Francis in his *Letter to the Rulers of the People*. His caustic prophecy to the town of Perugia for its unjust treatment of prisoners of Assisi taken in war, in particular, is altogether appropriate, given the Christian foundation that undergirded the medieval society of his day.

We can also point to the active resistance of the Lutheran theologian Dietrich Bonhoeffer to Nazism in the 1930s and 1940s to give historical precedence to Christian activism. Today in America we are ruled by a government that is not overtly Christian, but does invite the participation of its citizens. Therefore, we must be both obedient to government and responsible for the appropriate development of government. This applies not only to the world at large, but in a specific way to our nation and the local communities in which we live. At the same time, we should not take our eyes off our eventual homeland in heaven.

All of this impinges on our obedience to God. We should have at least some understanding of our approach to obeying government when seeking to live simply for God, because such living involves peace and social justice. Simple living means being committed to preferential treatment of the poor of the world—the poor not only within our inner cities, but also in the Third World. Our commitment to simplicity must spill over into the realms of politics and social action. Therefore, it's important for us to consider how we should relate to the political situations in which we find ourselves, so we can live out the call to simplicity of life.

More particularly, we are also called to obedience within the church. When we approach our Christian brothers and sisters with an attitude of humble obedience, we are actually expressing obedience to Christ. Because of the incarnation, we are interdependent. After all, our fellow Christian possesses the Spirit of God. As we submit in obedience to the church, its teachers and its teaching, we submit ourselves to God. The great mystery of the incarnation, the eternal wonder of Christ's presence on earth in his church, demands nothing less than total and unhesitating obedience to those over us. Thus, in our obedience to one another, in our submission to the teaching church, we submit to Christ and, through Christ, to the Father.

As we seek to live simple, humble, and obedient lives before God, it is comforting to know that through obedience to the church, we find a great hedge of safety keeping us from harm, from falsehood, and from deception. Our Lord promised that when the Spirit would come upon the church, she would be guided into all truth. The church is a divinely appointed guardian in whom we can trust totally. The opposite of obedience is rebellion, as the opposite of humility is pride. It was rebellion and pride which corrupted the greatest of all created beings, the archangel Lucifer.

In submitting to the church—which is guided and empowered by the Holy Spirit—we are submitting to the successors of the apostles. As such, we need to realize that though they are human, they nonetheless reflect Jesus as his delegated authority. From the earliest days of the church, we find recognition of this fact and submission to those in ecclesial positions of authority. Even St. Paul consulted with the church leadership in Jerusalem to be certain that the course of evangelism he was pursuing among the gentiles was not in vain. This is a powerful lesson to us, particularly in an age when criticism of church leadership and dissent from church teaching are commonly accepted and even encouraged in many quarters.

Submission to the church's authority and obedience to its teaching should never be oppressive. Yes, it can be difficult and challenging, but it should never be an experience of fear on our part, nor the capricious exercise of power on the part of leaders. Keeping in mind the focus of this book, humble submission and obedience will help to clarify many issues in our lives and simplify our day-to-day existence. Obedience to revealed truth will, in fact, help us to focus our thoughts and meditations on simple Christian living in the midst of our desperately complicated and confused world.

I can recall a story of obedience to my spiritual director. I had not been in the Catholic church for very long when my spiritual director not only encouraged me, but actually went so far as to command me, if at all possible, to go to the Holy Land to walk where Jesus walked. He said it would be good for my understanding of Scripture. I felt that I had a fairly good understanding of Scripture. My spiritual life was alive and well. My spirituality was based very strongly on the Gospels and in particular on the person of Jesus.

I did not see the wisdom in his advice, but I respected his authority over me. Since a trip to the Holy Land was possible, I went ahead and obeyed. Consequently, out of obedience to my spiritual director, I gained an insight into Scripture which has been invaluable to me in subsequent years. That trip gave me an insight into Scripture which I didn't even know I needed until *after* I obeyed.

For me, it was a great lesson in learning how to obey superiors. You learn to trust even when you don't understand exactly where they are heading with their instruction, trusting not so much in them, but in the Spirit of the living God who works through them. This kind of obedience does not bring death, it brings life.

As founder of the Brothers and Sisters of Charity and also as the spiritual father of the community, I am deeply appreciative of the direction the church provides. As the superior of an ecumenical community with a Catholic foundation, I have to submit myself to the covering and the leadership of the Catholic church. Admittedly, this can sometimes be painful and a real test of my faith. Yet I find many times that those who are in authority over me and those who are my spiritual elders save me even greater heartache through their counsel, their advice, and even their commands. Though I am the founder and the head of this community, I have to constantly remember that I do not have only a one-on-one relationship with Jesus. I have a relationship with Jesus through the church which places me in a healthy submission to those who in turn are over me—though they are not specifically a part of this community. This relationship has been the salvation of my own spiritual life time and again. It has also been very helpful in the leadership of this community. I know that I am not limited to relying on my own discernment, but I can seek the advice of those whom God has placed in leadership over me.

I am particularly interested in the Franciscan way of obedience which I find to be readily adaptable to Christian laity in every level of society. Franciscan obedience is based not on external dimensions of religious life or particular requirements found in canon law, but upon the internal law of love. As St. Paul said, "Love does no evil to the neighbor; hence, love is the fulfillment of the law" (Rom 13:10). Remember how Jesus himself responded when asked which of the commandments of the law was the greatest?

> "You shall love the Lord, your God, with all your heart, with all your soul, and with all your mind. This is the greatest and the first commandment. The second is like it: You shall love your neighbor as yourself. The whole law and the prophets depend on these two commandments." (Mt 22:37-40)

It is this kind of love which empowers us to seek and successfully foster an obedient attitude. It is far more motivational than any written prescription. Recall the words of Christ: "I tell you, unless your righteousness surpasses that of the scribes and Pharisees, you will not enter into the kingdom of heaven" (Mt 5:20). In a sense, love makes obedience automatic, which is the underlying thought in St. Augustine's famous quote: "Love God and do what you will."

Once again we look to that great Franciscan source, Thomas of Celano. In his *Second Life of St. Francis,* he writes,

> This is the perfect and highest obedience: take a lifeless body and place it where you will. It does not resist being moved, it does not murmur about its position. This is a truly obedient man; he does not ask why he is moved, he cares not where he is placed, he does not insist on being elsewhere. Raised to an office, he retains his accustomed humility; the more he is honored, the more unworthy does he consider himself.

The point is we should be dead to self and alive to Christ! Here we find the kind of mortification of ambition and detachment from self-will which makes one malleable under God's direction. This is what St. Francis called the total giving up of one's self to obedience. As long as we are "alive and kicking," obedience will be extremely difficult. If we persist in the fight to accomplish our own will, we will never truly yield to God, for it is only in the cross of Christ that we can truly find humble obedience. Francis would say that unless we consider ourselves dead, meditating upon this fact, we will never be able to be obedient to God or to his church in this world. We must each think of ourselves as lifeless bodies, dead to sin, dead to our ambitions, dead to the temptation to have our own way. Then we will find a whole new way of life that is truly free.

Jesus certainly did not mince words on this score: ". . . whoever does not take up his cross and follow after me is not worthy of me. Whoever finds his life will lose it, and whoever loses his life for my sake will find it" (Mt 10:38-39). This kind of total commitment can sound very frightening because it costs us everything. But look at the payoff! Jesus did not come into the world to overpower us or deprive us, he came to empower us and to bless us abundantly. As he said: "I came so that they might have life and have it more abundantly" (Jn 10:10).

The prideful desire to determine our own destiny can only produce sin which, as we know, brings forth death. Obedience, on the other hand, brings forth life. As Paul said to the Romans, ". . . just as through the disobedience of one person the many were made sinners, so through

the obedience of one the many will be made righteous"
(Rom 5:19). That one man of course, is Christ. Francis
understood, perhaps better than anyone else, that Christ
was God's expression of love to the world. Obedience,
therefore, becomes the result of our love response to God
and cannot be based on power, domination, legalities, or
manipulation.

What happens, we might ask, when a leader in the
church or in a religious community is not living a godly
life or abuses authority? Jesus answered this question by
distinguishing between the *person* of the successor to
Moses and the *office* of the successor to Moses. He urged
his disciples to follow their religious leaders' commands
but not their personal example (Mt 23:1-3). St. Francis
continued this teaching within his own order and even
went so far as to place himself in submission to the least
experienced of all brothers. Obviously, he did not place
himself in submission and obedience to the person, but to
Christ, which makes all the difference. It goes without
saying that this kind of radical obedience to authority can
sometimes be painful as conflict and dissent emerge.
However, it is through suffering that we draw closer to
Christ. It is by the crucifixion of our own desires that we
are raised up in power with Jesus into abundant life and
joy.

There's another way God has ordained to check abuses
of authority among his people. We know that he provided
an apostolic structure—a continuing chain of authority
which defines and spreads the teaching of the church. But
God also has created a prophetic structure which will
sometimes challenge or confirm the apostolic structure,

thereby creating a way to call leaders to task for wrong-doing or an abuse of power.

There are some important differences between the two structures. The apostolic structure of the New Testament church is often traceable through the apostolic succession seen fully in the bishops and their delegated clergy of priests and deacons, much like the levitical priesthood of the Old Testament. But in both the Old and New Testaments, the prophetic structure is like the wind of the Spirit which raises up prophets, regardless of their visible place in any organized structure or institution, even in legitimate religion.

Recall the Old Testament prophets who, although they were lifted up by God to call Israel to repentance, were not necessarily of the Levitical priesthood. Such was the case with Elijah, and even the great prophet Samuel who, like the priests, offered up sacrifice although he was not of a priestly clan. Jeremiah called the priests and the prophets alike to account for wrongdoing and faced persecution from the religious establishment. Nathan the prophet rebuked David the king for his sins of adultery and murder. Jesus himself in the New Testament minced no words with the scribes and the Pharisees, even though they held legitimate positions of religious authority.

This same model flowed into the early church and has come down to the present day. Remember the occasion when Peter, although he was clearly recognized as the leading authority in the early church, was confronted by Paul, even to the point of Paul stating that Peter "clearly was wrong" (Gal 2:11)? But we also know that Paul submitted himself to Peter, James, and John when he came to Jerusalem to seek their counsel (Acts 15:1-2). Here we see an example of a prophetic model being perfected through dialogue, respect, and balance with church leaders.

MODELS OF OBEDIENCE

Why, the reader might now be asking, are we giving so much ink to the concept of obedience in a book on simplicity? The answer, in my opinion, comes from the experience of life, not from theory or theology. It is the experience of those who have lived the simple life most radically which compels us to examine their obedience and derive some insight from their example. It is no accident of history that St. Francis of Assisi, St. Benedict, St. Theresa of Avila, and many other great Christian saints have certain things in common. The simplicity of their lives was matched only by the humble, persistent obedience they expressed to God and to the church.

Consider the modern example of Mother Teresa of Calcutta. She lives a life of true gospel poverty, and her international exploits in serving the poor and dying around the world are now legendary. She has become, ironically, one of this generation's most noted humanitarians and sought-after lecturers. Her books are read by millions and even the cynical press are enthralled with her. Yet she is unquestioning in her total obedience to the Catholic church. The connection between simplicity and obedience seems pervasive among those who stand out as towering examples of faith.

It is also important to note that the many movements spawned by great church leaders have attracted not only priests, monks, nuns, brothers, and sisters, but also lay men and women and their entire families. Simple living, humility, and obedience are not goals to be achieved only by saints or super-Christians. They are available to us all if we will but yield ourselves totally to Christ, with a willingness to begin a pilgrimage toward him, ever deepening our faith along the way.

The first step is simple: we must desire to embark upon this journey. As St. Paul says, "For God is the one who, for his good purpose, works in you both to desire and to work" (Phil 2:13). Our subsequent efforts will be met, at times, with setbacks and perhaps even suffering. Old habits and entrenched behavior require time to change. But don't despair! The fact that you are reading this book is evidence that God is already offering you the gift of simplicity. Now you must respond.

God provides direction through the teaching authority of the church and also dispenses graces through her to help us persevere. When viewed properly, these teachings become a great blessing and a wonderful help as we seek to live simply. God's instruction, through his church, becomes tracks on which we can move forward like a train, but only if we are obedient. Our lives can flow with purpose and direction like the river described earlier in this chapter, but only if we allow the banks to channel and direct us. Obedience, then, becomes a life-giving discipline and an opportunity. Through mature, thoughtful submission to authority, we discover that we can begin to simplify our lives.

But how does obedience make sense in the real world? The world issues we face are complex and complicated. They threaten the very existence of the civilized world as we know it. The arms race, global poverty, and the holocaust of abortion can seem to be complex knots that are virtually impossible for an isolated individual to untie.

The church—in her collective wisdom guided by the Spirit, the successors to the apostles, and the prophets from within her own ranks—helps to provide some clear answers. As a Roman Catholic Christian, I am proud of the fact that both the Catholic church and various other Christian denominations have raised their voices prophetically to speak to the troubles of our world.

The primary problems the churches are addressing prophetically include pro-life issues, the nuclear arms race, and concern for the poorest of the poor. Out of these flow the many other concerns of our society, such as the perversion of sexual ethics and the crass, materialistic consumerism which eats away not only at our society, but the whole world as well. Of course, behind all these issues stands the more primary concern for every individual: conversion of heart to a personal love relationship with Jesus Christ as Lord. I am grateful and proud that the very church established by Christ himself continues to speak with the same prophetic authority about these issues and the primacy of the gospel. We should heed that prophetic call with a response of obedience.

I am grateful that God raises up from within the church itself prophetic voices and prophetic communities. This prophetic raising up is a work of the Spirit within the church. Even by canon law, the church itself is morally obliged to be open to these prophetic voices which address possible corruptions and problems in the more institutional expressions of the church.

Ultimately, a proper understanding of our obedience to this prophetic voice and the authority it serves can help lead us to a true and proper simplicity of life. This simplicity calls us to be childlike, not childish. Therefore, a full understanding of obedience to proper guidance is necessary if we are to have a mature experience of simplicity. This obedience involves primarily obedience to God; secondly, to the church and her leadership; thirdly, to all humanity in its various expressions of government; and fourthly, even to all creation itself. Again, this obedience is not unconditional, nor is it blind. We go into this obedience with our eyes wide open and with mature understanding, knowing that it is this humble obedience which leads us to true simplicity of life.

Practical Pointers on Growing in Obedience

1) Can you claim to be humble yet be habitually disobedient to those over you? Why is this a contradiction in terms?

2) Name some ways everyone should be obedient to civil and religious authority. Are there times when it is appropriate to disobey such authority? Where and when? Under what conditions?

3) How does the prophetic role of simple living fit into the church's call to be a witness to the world? How

can obedience to the church make you a prophet of Jesus Christ?

4) Think of some specific way you can respond to the call to be obedient to God and others in authority over you. Put it into practice in your daily life.

THREE

The Power of Prayer and Meditation

INNER ATTITUDES REALLY DO affect the way we think and live our lives. We have seen that humility and obedience, for example, can have far-reaching consequences in our lives. They can lead to a simple, focused Christian life that bears fruit in our personal lives, in the church, and even touches our world. It is from just such inner attitudes of the heart that our behavior—and its many untold consequences—is formed.

In boldly condemning the scribes and Pharisees as frauds, Jesus staked out the priorities for our internal world as Christians. He knew that while their appearances and external duties indicated cleanliness and order, they were, in actual fact, evil within—"like whitewashed tombs" (Mt 23:27). Our interior lives must be examined and reviewed by Christ. It is upon this foundation that our external lives will bear genuine fruit, allowing us to bring forth peace, justice, evangelization, and lifestyles consistent with our Christian identity.

How does this process begin? How does Christ enter our innermost being? We know from Scripture that the Holy Spirit, the Paraclete summoned by Jesus to comfort and guide his church (Jn 14:16-17, 26), abides within us (Jn 15:26; 16:7-15). As St. Paul wrote, we actually become children of God in a spirit of adoption through which we cry out, "Abba!" (Rom 8:14-16). This Spirit is poured out on all Christians, and it is in the Holy Spirit that we proclaim Jesus as Lord (1 Cor 12:3). It is the Holy Spirit who helps us in our weaknesses, teaching us to pray, even making intercession for us, "with inexpressible groanings" (Rom 8:26-27).

This Spirit leads us into prayer and meditation in God's presence, revealing God the Father and his Son to us. Unfortunately, meditation is a concept which now carries negative connotations for many, because of its misuse at the hands of disreputable spiritual leaders and even cultists. While we must take care when preparing to engage in meditation, we must not allow ourselves to be intimidated by counterfeits. Again, it is important to take a look at the Scriptures where we find St. Paul writing in Romans 12:2, "Do not conform yourself to this age but be transformed by the renewal of your mind, that you may discern what is the will of God, what is good and pleasing and perfect." And remember the famous scriptural adage, "As a man thinketh in his heart, so is he." Clearly, there is a strong connection between thoughts and actions, attitudes and behavior. Therefore, how important it is that we seek God in prayer and meditate on his attributes and Word. Such prayer and meditation provides the clarity, strength, and simplicity our lives otherwise sorely lack.

St. Paul urges us in the fourth chapter of Philippians to direct our thoughts to "whatever is true, whatever is honorable, whatever is just, whatever is pure, whatever is lovely, whatever is gracious" (v. 8). This kind of focus can require discipline as we attempt to "take every thought captive in obedience to Christ" (2 Cor 10:5). In Ephesians 4:22-24, Paul writes,

> . . . you should put away the old self of your former way of life, corrupted through deceitful desires, and be renewed in the spirit of your minds, and put on the new self, created in God's way in righteousness and holiness of truth.

In other words, we die to our old way of life, and then we are resurrected to a new way of living in Christ. We acquire a whole new way of thinking!

Authentic Christian meditation affects our thoughts and produces an entirely new outlook on life. We die to our old desires and thoughts and find real new life in Christ. We are literally born again. And it all begins with our thoughts.

In order to align our attitudes with God's will, we must allow the Holy Spirit clear access to our inner life. Once the Spirit is indwelling us, we must allow him to be stirred up in a way which brings healthy spiritual change and growth. But how is this done?

HOW DO WE VIEW CREATION?

We may begin by looking to all of creation in prayerful meditation because, as Thomas a' Kempis says in *The Imitation of Christ*, "If we are pure and holy within, all of creation will become for us as a book of the knowledge and the goodness of God." As we previously stated, St. Francis also had deep love and respect for creation which he learned to read as if it were a holy book from God. He saw creation as art, and he therefore praised the divine artist. It was through creation's life-giving reason and cause that St. Francis rejoiced in the Lord. It was in beautiful things that he saw divine beauty. He saw the footprints of Jesus in creation, and "he followed his beloved everywhere; he made for himself from all things a ladder by which to come even to God's throne" (Thomas of Celano's *Second Life of St. Francis*).

St. Paul wrote in Romans 1:20: ". . . since the creation of the world, his invisible attributes of eternal power and divinity have been able to be understood and perceived in what he has made." The psalmist in Psalm 104 says, "How manifold are your works, O LORD!/In wisdom you have wrought them all—/the earth is full of your creatures" (v. 24). Consider the Gospels: Jesus frequently used natural images throughout his teachings. He was quick to take lessons from the birds of the air or the lilies of the field, from wheat which provides sustenance, from the olive tree or the fig tree.

I believe it is fair to say that if we seek guidance for our meditation upon God, we need only to look creation to find God's traces everywhere. At times, when we are earnestly seeking God, it is possible that we might find expressions of his wisdom by simply taking a walk through a park or in the woods. It is this wisdom which guides us in our meditations upon God who is, finally, the most simple being in all the universe.

WHAT ROLE SHOULD SCRIPTURE HAVE IN OUR PRAYER LIFE?

Spiritual reading, particularly the Scriptures, also helps to direct our thoughts and our minds toward God. The Scriptures represent the most trustworthy and sure source of divine teaching. The psalmist wrote in Psalm 1, "Happy the man who follows not/the counsel of the wicked/ . . . But delights in the law of the LORD/and meditates on his law day and night" (Ps 1:1-2). Meditation on the Scripture gives new life and direction to the human soul as the psalmist wrote of the person who meditates on Scripture in Psalm 1: "He is like a tree/planted near running water,/That yields its fruit in due season,/and whose leaves never fade" (v. 3).

In John 14:26, we are reminded by Jesus that "The advocate, the holy Spirit that the Father will send in my name—he will teach you everything and remind you of all that [I] told you." As was discussed earlier, the Holy Spirit is invited into our innermost beings. In a subjective way, he guides and leads us. He reminds us of Christ's teaching—a gift of guidance provided to every Christian in the Spirit. But does this mean that because we are provided with an indwelling guide we no longer need specific teaching or instruction from the church? Absolutely not!

It is important that a balance be struck between the subjective and the objective. Believers need to understand that God has appointed teaching authority through the ages, beginning with the apostles, and we must obey this teaching as from Christ. After all, it was Jesus himself who commissioned the apostles to teach the nations, saying,

> "All power in heaven and on earth has been given to me. Go, therefore, and make disciples of all nations, baptizing them in the name of the Father, and of the Son, and of the holy Spirit, teaching them to observe all that I have commanded you. And behold, I am with you always, until the end of the age." (Mt 28:18-20)

And remember Paul's words in 1 Corinthians 12:28 when he reminded believers that ". . . God has designated in the church to be: first, apostles; second, prophets; third, teachers." In the fourth chapter of Ephesians, Paul also outlines roles of service for the faithful with apostles charged as leaders and as authorized teachers in the body of Christ.

It is part of God's plan that we come to fully understand and appreciate the authority of the Scriptures in our lives. Remember that in the earliest days of the church there were no New Testament Scriptures. These early Christians had to rely on the teaching authority of the apostles. Not only had Jesus commissioned them as teaching authorities, but he had deposited with them the faith which would be transmitted within the church for all time. Members of the early church "devoted themselves to the teaching of the apostles" (Acts 2:42). Because the apostles were looked to as authorities in the growing body of Christ, all kinds of controversies and questions were put before them as they arose throughout the broader Christian community.

As local Christian communities outgrew the apostles' ability to pastor them individually, it was only natural that these divinely appointed teachers should use the prevailing medium of the day: written texts. Quite simply, letters were sent instructing Christians on how they should behave, and frequently specific questions of faith and morals were addressed. Gradually, a number of these letters were preserved and adopted by the church as inspired Scripture.

As the first generation of apostolic authority began to die out, orally transmitted histories of Jesus' ministry were also committed to writing and spread throughout the church in the form of the Gospels. The authority of Christ's life and teachings as well as the instructions of apostolic leaders were thus combined in the Gospels and the Epistles to create one of God's greatest gifts to the church, the Scriptures of the New Testament. It is this living and dynamic authority of the New Testament as the Word of God that gives the Christian extraordinary insight and guidance. The church, authorized by Jesus himself, embodied his teachings in the written word with such power that it "is living and effective, sharper than any two-edged sword, penetrating even between soul and spirit, joints and marrow, and able to discern reflections and thoughts of the heart" (Heb 4:12).

Obviously, the Scriptures should hold a very important place in our lives as we attempt to discern the proper approach to simplicity. In reading the Scriptures and prayerfully meditating upon them, we are actually tapping into authorized apostolic documents which draw their life from Christ himself. The Scriptures become, in a sense, an opportunity to reconsider our roots and origins as a people of God who continue their pilgrimage toward him, his Word serving as our compass.

Care must be taken, though, that the Scriptures not be studied in isolation from the ongoing teaching of the church. True, we have the Spirit of God within us to guide and direct us. We have an objective body of teaching in the Scriptures. But remember: it was the church that authenticated these Scriptures, and it is the teaching office of the church which provides the commentary or the instruction to interpret these biblical documents. A balance must be maintained between tradition and Scripture.

As the *Dogmatic Constitution on Divine Revelation* from the Second Vatican Council teaches:

> There exist a close connection and communication between sacred Tradition and sacred Scripture. For both of them, flowing from the same divine wellspring, in a certain way merge into a unity and tends toward the same end ... Sacred Tradition and sacred Scripture form one sacred deposit of the Word of God which is entrusted to the Church. ... (Sections 9, 10)

We are further taught in Vatican II that the task of correctly interpreting the Scriptures has been handed down through the living, teaching office of the church, which is composed of the bishops united to the pope, Peter's successor. Of course, this teaching office is not above the Word of God, but serves the Word of God. The teaching office guards it, faithfully explains it to the faithful, and serves as a kind of holy custodian of the written Word.

St. Francis understood the healthy balance of sacred tradition, the Scriptures, and the working of the Holy Spirit in a way which produced a full, yet simple faith. While he encouraged the study of the Scriptures, he did not want the accumulation of knowledge to undermine humility and poverty of spirit. He desired that the study of Scripture be a meditation for the Franciscan brothers in such a way that their lives were truly changed by growing in simplicity and in their ability to preach the Word of God. Historical evidence clearly shows that St. Francis of Assisi relied heavily on the Scriptures as evidenced in his Rules, the founding documents of the Franciscan Order. However, he never approached Scripture in such a way that made it complicated, overly sophisticated, or theologically complex. He approached it in a way that was prayerful, virtuous, and simple.

Ultimately, for St. Francis, the Scriptures became a means to an end—that end being the possession of scriptural principles within his heart and soul, and the outworking of this interior treasure in a lived faith. Toward the end of his life when he was extremely ill, one of the brothers came to Francis, concerned about his suffering and pain, asking, "Would you like me to read you some Scripture to bring comfort to your soul?" Francis responded, "It is good to read the testimonies of Scripture; it is good to seek the Lord God in them. As for me, however, I have already made so much of Scripture my own that I have more than enough to meditate on and revolve in my mind. I need no more; I know Christ, the poor crucified one . . . what need is there for more words? Let us come to deeds" (Thomas of Celano, *Second Life of St. Francis*).

I recommend that those who truly desire to live a simple life meditate on the Scriptures daily and in particular on the life of Jesus Christ. Pray and meditate on the daily Scripture readings of the liturgy. Take time aside in a quiet place to meditate on God as he reveals himself through the words of sacred Scripture.

THE IMPORTANCE OF PRAYER DEVOTIONS

The Old and New Testament Scriptures were created in substantially illiterate cultures. Only the priests, rabbis, and other ranking leaders actually knew how to read and write. For the most part, the Jewish laity and later the average early Christian did not know how to read or write, so they listened to the reading of their Scriptures and to commentary upon the Scriptures. Even had they been able to read and study their holy writings, individual manuscripts were so rare that they were effectively beyond the means of the average person to obtain.

Therefore, over a period of time, oral transmission of the Scriptures developed from generation to generation. Consequently, the Jewish people in ancient Israel used memorized devotional prayers more than actual reading in the expression of their faith.

This is also true of the New Testament church. As the church grew in the early centuries A.D., it encountered cultures where writing and reading were more widespread. But even in Europe obtaining copies of manuscripts was far beyond the means of the average lay person. Believers therefore memorized Scriptures, prayers, and the teachings of their faith. It was a very simple and humble way of maintaining faith in a nonintellectual era. In fact, it embodied St. Paul's injunction to the Romans to "not be haughty but associate with the lowly; do not be wise in your own estimation" (Rom 12:16).

Jesus said, ". . . unless you turn and become like children, you will not enter the kingdom of heaven" (Mt 18:3). We should be careful not to reject the wealth of devotional prayers and practices which were handed down to us as children. While I have read and studied much in these past few years, I can honestly say that I have never found more rich and balanced prayers and meditations than those handed to me as a child: the Our Father, the Apostle's Creed, simple bedtime prayers, and prayers before meals. They all represent a treasure of simple, religious truths on which we can always call. They frequently bring a sense of simplicity, serenity, and focus back into my own life as I prayerfully recite them.

Let us examine more specifically some prayers which have weathered the test of time. The Rosary, both Eastern

Orthodox and Roman Catholic, is one such example. It was common practice in the early church for Christians to pause three times daily to recite either privately or corporately the Lord's Prayer or the Our Father. When our Lord's followers requested his teaching on prayer, this simple prayer was his direct response and has been treasured by the church ever since. It is recited at every Mass around the world daily. The prayer is profound yet extraordinarily simple. Of course, the Lord's Prayer or the Our Father is a central prayer in the devotion of the Rosary.

In the early centuries of the church, disputes arose regarding the nature of Christ and the Trinity. In direct proclamation of the trinitarian mystery of the one true God, another prayer was born: the "Glory Be." Again, the prayer is very simple but has endured the test of time and is repeated by the church on many occasions: "Glory be to the Father, and to the Son, and to the Holy Spirit, as it was in the beginning, is now, and ever shall be, world without end. Amen." In that simple expression we speak of the deepest of mystical and theological truths. If we center on the simplicity of this prayer, we begin to appreciate the profound reality of God's trinitarian nature. Again, this is a prayer which is included in the Rosary.

The Rosary developed out of monastic prayer where monks daily prayed the 150 psalms. The entire Psalter was committed to memory and prayed by the monks. Lay people, inspired by this monastic practice, also desired to pray the psalms but did not have access to the Psalter and instead developed the practice of carrying 150 small stones, one for each psalm. The small stones served as counting aids and were handled one by one as the prayers were said. Over a period of time, the Rosary developed as a prayer practice and took varying forms in the East and West of Christendom.

The Marian emphasis of Rosary prayer came after the Council of Ephesus in A.D. 431 in which Mary was declared to be the *Theotokus* or the Mother of God, a declaration meant to firmly establish the truth of Christ's deity. Mary's role in salvation history was further highlighted by recognizing her as a model of the church, a true example of faith, and a prototype of the Christian disciple.

In the Western church, the faithful began to recite a Hail Mary for each of the 150 psalms and gradually began to use beads on a string, instead of pebbles in a pouch. Eventually, the 150 beads became groupings of fifteen larger beads or decades, each decade being focused on a particular mystery in the lives of Jesus and his mother. Subsequently, the Our Father was added at the beginning of each decade of Hail Marys, and a Glory Be at the end of each decade. This prayer form was popularized by St. Dominic and the Dominicans in the thirteenth and fourteenth centuries.

Through the development of history and in different disciplines and regions, Rosary prayers evolved in different directions. The Franciscan Crown, for example, was a version of the Rosary with seven decades. It emphasizes the incarnational, the joyful, and the glorious aspects of the life of Jesus Christ and the life of the church as represented in the person of Mary. It was also at this point in history that the final part of the Hail Mary was added. Up until that time, the prayer went simply, "Hail Mary, full of grace, the Lord is with thee. Blessed are thou among women and blessed is the fruit of thy womb, Jesus." This, of course, is taken directly from Scripture.

After the time of the Franciscan Crown, however, the prayer was extended to read, "Holy Mary, Mother of God, pray for us sinners now and at the hour of our death." This was a further elaboration upon the role of Mary not only as the mother of Jesus, but as the Mother of God, highlighting the deity of Jesus. In recent years, we have seen the development of the Scriptural Rosary. In addition to the simple, memorized prayers, particular Scriptures recount the story of each mystery.

Personally, I have found praying the Rosary to be one of the most powerful tools I possess in obtaining simple, childlike meditation on the life of Jesus Christ from the perspective of a member of the church, the bride of Christ symbolized by Mary. The joyful, sorrowful, and glorious mysteries all provide a way for me to visualize in my mind the life of Jesus without having to study volumes of reading material. I simply pray as a child. It was at a time of trial and tribulation in my own life that God directed me to this Rosary prayer discipline. I was searching for a new level of simplification, and it was the prayer of the Rosary which focused my mind, producing healing and filling me with the wonders of contemplation and a mystical prayer experience. I can recommend no other prayer more highly than this devotional prayer.

There are many examples of devotional practices which have evolved in the long history of the church, so many of which provide a simple focus on our Lord. From Franciscan tradition I can immediately think of two other devotional practices which have spread throughout the entire world from humble beginnings.

The first is the Christmas Crib or the Nativity Scene. It was not until the time of St. Francis that the reenactment of Christ's birth began to develop in the church. St. Francis was filled with great love and joy at the thought of the incarnation. He understood that we need, at times, vivid representations from the life of Jesus to focus more clearly on this event which proved so decisive for all of humankind. Francis and his brother friars created a scene where a manger was prepared, an ox and a donkey were stationed nearby, brothers sang praises to the Lord, and the night resounded in rejoicing at the memory of Christ's birth. Mass was celebrated over the manger, and the nativity reenactment began a tradition which spread around the world and can be seen even today in Christmas celebrations worldwide. The simple devotion of one man, St. Francis, resulted in a blessed reenactment of the incarnation which is now practiced by hundreds of millions.

In the eighteenth century, Leonard of Port Maurice instituted the Way of the Cross at the hermitage of Font Colombo in Italy. This particular devotion reenacted the path Jesus walked toward his crucifixion. Based primarily on Scripture, it also includes some other long-held traditions. The Way of the Cross is emphasized during Lent in churches which observe the liturgical calendar. You can find the Way of the Cross—also called the Stations of the Cross—on the walls of almost any Roman Catholic church around the world.

I hope these examples of devotional practices illustrate

the principle that simple prayer in the life of the believer may be focused and enhanced by using devotional traditions and disciplines which draw us back to Jesus. None of the devotions are so complex that they are hard to learn. They are not beyond the imagination of even the smallest child. Thus, we prune back the complexities of our sophisticated learning and enter into that childlike knowledge of the gospel through the use of a simple devotion. I have found these devotional practices to be an essential part of a simple lifestyle.

THE CHARISMATIC DIMENSION IN PRAYER: A GIFT OF FREEDOM IN THE SPIRIT

One of the most simple and childlike ways to pray is through the active stirring up of the charismatic gifts, in particular the gift of tongues. Through charismatic prayer, we stir up very intentionally and particularly the work of the Holy Spirit within us.

All Christians need to be empowered by the Holy Spirit. Consider the apostles—though they had sat at the feet of the greatest spiritual teacher ever, though they had witnessed miracles and seen the risen Christ, they required the kind of empowerment that fell upon them at Pentecost. Experience and knowledge were not enough. Jesus told them, after his resurrection, not to leave Jerusalem, but to wait for the fulfillment of his Father's promise. That promise was empowerment by the Holy Spirit. Then they would go forth as witnesses in Jerusalem, throughout Judea and Samaria, and to the very ends of the earth. Indeed, the apostles and other followers of Jesus were empowered at Pentecost by the Holy Spirit and that same power is available to us today.

How do we receive this Spirit of God? In Luke 11:9-13, Jesus said:

> "Ask and you will receive; seek and you will find; knock and the door will be opened to you. For everyone who asks, receives; and the one who seeks, finds; and to the one who knocks, the door will be opened. What father among you would hand his son a snake when he asks for a fish? Or hand him a scorpion when he asks for an egg? If you then, who are wicked, know how to give good gifts to your children, how much more will the Father in heaven give the holy Spirit to those who ask him?"

We know that the Holy Spirit has already been given to everyone who calls upon the name of the Lord, that is, to all Christians. Yet there remains the question of stirring up that Spirit within our lives. Paul wrote in 2 Timothy 1:6-7, "I remind you to stir into flame the gift of God that you have through the imposition of my hands. For God did not give us a spirit of cowardice . . ." This means there is something more than simply possessing God's Spirit— it must be released in a powerul new way.

The Holy Spirit comes to us in many different ways. The Spirit is given to us at baptism, at confirmation, through the reception of all the sacraments, and each time we hear the Word of God proclaimed. The Spirit is offered to us regularly when we receive the Lord in the Eucharist.

But the fact remains that the Spirit of God can operate beyond these avenues. The Spirit is a gift which is offered, but it can only benefit us if we receive it.

It is much like the experience of birth. A child is born into this world through no choice of its own. The child is conceived by the choice of the mother and father and by the grace of the life-giving God. Likewise, in its mother's womb, it is nurtured and it grows. When the time for birth comes, the child really has very little to say about it! The gift of life is simply given as a grace. But once the child is born, life begins as a maturing process and choices must be made—choices which ultimately determine whether life continues. The child needs to eat and breathe, and it must be taken care of.

And so it is with the Holy Spirit. The Spirit is given to us by our parents and by a believing faith community at baptism and at various other sacramental and liturgical points in our life. In a sense, we can say that we have very little choice about it. But once this gift has been given, we must then decide how to use the gift. It is possible that we could actually reject the gift or ignore it.

Although we do experience various levels of giftedness from the Holy Spirit in our lives, we must be encouraged. As St. Paul encouraged Timothy: "stir into flame the gift of God . . ." (2 Tm 1:6). So how do we stir up this gift? The psalmist gives us the beginning of an answer to this question in Psalm 100:4, "Enter his gates with thanksgiving,/his courts with praise." I believe that praise and thanksgiving are vital keys in unleashing the kind of empowerment God would have for us in his Spirit. And I believe it is exactly what St. Paul was describing when he wrote in Ephesians 5:18-20:

> . . . be filled with the Spirit, addressing one another [in] psalms and hymns and spiritual songs, singing and playing to the Lord in your hearts, giving thanks always and for everything in the name of our Lord Jesus Christ to God the Father.

I will be the first to admit that praise and thanksgiving before God are not always easy. Frequently, due to difficult circumstances in our lives, or emotional impediments, we just don't feel like singing, praising, or thanking God. This is where we must enter into praise and thanksgiving not by feelings, but by faith! Faith, like love, is an act of the will—it is a decision. Once the decision has been made to praise God and to thank him, something happens. Our heart responds and, eventually, our emotions will follow our will.

One of the best scriptural illustrations of offering thanksgiving and praise to God in spite of circumstances is found in Habakkuk 3:17-19. The conditions in which Habakkuk finds himself would seem to produce anything but a thankful attitude or praise. Yet, the prophet knows in his heart by faith that God will never abandon him, saying,

> For though the fig tree blossom not
>   nor fruit be on the vines,
> Though the yield of the olive fail
>   and the terraces produce no nourishment,

Though the flocks disappear from the fold
    and there be no herd in the stalls,
Yet will I rejoice in the LORD
    and exult in my saving God.
GOD, my Lord, is my strength;
    he makes my feet swift as those of hinds
    and enables me to go up on the heights.

A better example of praising, thanking, and rejoicing in God by faith in the face of adversity can be found nowhere in the Scriptures. Such an example serves to motivate us in stirring up the power of the Holy Spirit by an act of our will—God wants us to be a people of praise and thanksgiving.

Of course there will be times when our emotions and overwhelming circumstances will make praise and thanksgiving an extremely difficult proposition. There will be times when we feel so down and out that the simple act of praying or thinking about the Lord seems beyond our grasp. It could be fear, anger, grief, physical or emotional pain—or a combination of these feelings—which become a barrier to free expression of thanks and praise.

At times, we may be on a downward spiral of negativity. But praise and thanksgiving can reverse this plunge and help us experience an upward spiral of inspiration, faith, and victory. In fact, it is precisely at this point that God has given us a tool to unlock the door to praise and thanksgiving: pure prayer of the Holy Spirit without precepts, concepts, conditions, or even understanding. It is a yielding to God in a kind of communication which cannot be defined in limited human terms.

St. Paul explained in Romans 8:26-27 how the Spirit assists us in our weakness and he even intercedes for us "with inexpressible groanings."

The gift of tongues—the language of the Spirit—is not understood in purely human terms. Rather, it is a language which expresses the deepest things of God. Though at first it may seem like foolishness to the uninitiated, in truth it is a mysterious, hidden wisdom, as Paul teaches in 1 Corinthians 2:6-9. I firmly believe there is a psychological principle involved with the gift of tongues. We can actually renew our mind and our emotions through using this gift which bypasses logical thought processes.

It is precisely at times when we seem incapable of prayer that our spirits must go directly to the Spirit of God. We direct our prayer and concerns to the source of all life without attempting to force them through the limits of human language.

Sometimes this involves (external) silence. Other times, however, it involves the principle that speaking not only symbolizes, but effects and makes real internal reality. We literally speak inner realities into existence. At such a time, we pray spirit to spirit, heart to heart with God. By doing so we bypass the mind in order to free ourselves of the clutter of our thoughts and emotions. Thus we experience praise, thanksgiving, and worship of God in a way which is utterly and absolutely beyond our human abilities of objectivity and reason. We pray in nonconceptualized words, speaking forth that which is in the very depths of our spirit and causing it to spread throughout the rest of our soul. Amazingly, we find that our troubled emotions—whether they be fear, anger, or confusion—are simply cast out of our heart. Once the mind clears and we can use it again, we are able to verbalize our praise and thanksgiving in intelligible human speech.

Sometimes the gift of tongues is not used to stir up the Spirit within, but is used to speak forth in the assembly, to stir up the Spirit within others. Tongues, therefore, is a charismatic gift for the individual and for the whole church. Of the more private gift, St. Paul says in 1 Corinthians 14:2-4:

> For one who speaks in a tongue does not speak to human beings but to God, for no one listens; he utters mysteries in spirit. On the other hand, one who prophesies does speak to human beings, for their building up, encouragement, and solace. Whoever speaks in a tongue builds himself up, but whoever prophesies builds up the church.

Paul then goes on to speak of the more public ministry of tongues:

> . . . I should like all of you to speak in tongues, but even more to prophesy. One who prophesies is greater than one who speaks in tongues, unless he interprets, so that the church may be built up (1 Cor 14:5).

St. Paul goes on to teach that a publicly spoken tongue should be interpreted through the gift of interpretation so that all might be edified (1 Cor 14:13, 27-28).

I'm always amazed by the number of Christians who do not seem to understand tongues. I am even more perplexed to find how many Christians flatly refuse to accept it. The historical and biblical reality of tongues during the very birth of the church is clearly depicted in Acts 2:1-7:

> When the time for Pentecost was fulfilled, they were all in one place together. And suddenly there came from the sky a noise like a strong driving wind, and it filled the entire house in which they were. Then there appeared to them tongues as of fire, which parted and came to rest on each one of them. And they were all filled with the holy Spirit and began to speak in different tongues, as the Spirit enabled them to proclaim.
>
> Now there were devout Jews from every nation under heaven staying in Jerusalem. At this sound, they gathered in a large crowd, but they were confused because each one heard them speaking in his own language. They were astounded. . . .

This was not an isolated event but occurred subsequently among believers in the early church and continues to this day. It is my strong belief that God would have most Christians benefit from this wondrous gift, yet many refuse out of ignorance or, worse, out of pride. At times we tend to want God and his gifts on our terms, which grieves the Spirit and precludes our full participation in God's blessings. We must be childlike and simple enough to hunger after whatever gifts God wishes to give us. We must be humble, obedient, simple. I explain the charismatic dimension of our faith in more detail in my book, *Regathering Power* (Servant Publications: Ann Arbor, Michigan, 1987).

To experience the charismatic gift of tongues, you must become as a child. In a sense, you must become a fool, letting go of every possession and allowing God to become your only wealth. The gift of tongues, I find, is an excellent way for the Christian to allow the simplicity of a child to emerge, so that we may learn the great mysteries of the kingdom of God that are beyond the wisest of the wise in our world. Will all experience this gift? No, they will not. But all of us must be simple and childlike enough to be willing to accept any gift from God. Such gifts are given according to his will, not our own.

The charismatic gifts have been experienced by various renewal movements throughout the ages, including the Franciscan movement from which I have learned so much. These gifts were characteristic of the Jesus movement and the charismatic renewal movement of the late '60s and early '70s. Even as I write, it has been widely prophesied that God is preparing to pour out a fresh Pentecostal wave of the Spirit upon the people of God, a far more powerful renewal than we have seen in many years. I believe this outpouring will be reflected in the radical, simple lives of those who experience the power of the Spirit. We cannot truly deal with simplicity unless we look at this charismatic dimension of our spiritual lives, because this power of the Spirit can help us overcome the materialism and the complexities of this age which minister death and depression throughout the entire world.

CONTEMPLATION: OUR UNION WITH GOD

Contemplation, properly understood, is capable of lifting our souls to spiritual heights. St. Bonaventure discussed the rapture and ecstasy which can be attained through contemplation in his writings, *On the Perfection of Life*:

Devotion may sometimes cause our spirit to "lose hold of itself and rise above itself"; to pass into a state of rapture: when we are enflamed with the ardour of such celestial desire that the whole world seems bitter and tiresome. The flame of intimate love, grown beyond human measure, makes the soul to swoon, to melt like wax, and to rise aloft like incense, higher and higher, to the very summit ... Again, in rapture sometimes the grace occurs because of the height of admiration "when our soul is of contemplation" irradiated with divine light, and held in suspense by the wonder of supreme beauty, it is thrown off its foundation. In the likeness of a flash of lightning, the deeper the soul is cast into the abyss by the contrast between beauty and itself, the higher and faster does it rise to the sublime ... Finally, rapture may come about through the height of exaltation ... our soul completely forgets what it is and what it was and its whole being becomes supernatural desire.

Here, through the cross, we can see Bonaventure passing from devotion to contemplation, all in mystical simplicity. "If you wish to know how such things come about," he wrote, "consult grace, not doctrine; desire, not understanding; prayerful groaning, not studious reading; the spouse, not the teacher; God, not man; darkness, not clarity."

St. Augustine said in his Confessions, "Nothing more simple than you can be found." He was speaking of God. He continued saying, "You alone are simple." St. Augustine was focusing on God and his profound simplicity, a reality on which we should all contemplate. The end of all Christian experience, the goal for which we all strive and, ultimately, the purest and simplest of all pursuits in the Christian life is union with God. Contemplation is a practice by which we may approach this union.

St. Symeon, the New Theologian, speaks of the simplicity of contemplative union with God, saying,

He comes with a certain image, but it is an image of God; for God could not appear under any image or figure; but he makes himself seen in his simplicity, formed in light without form, incomprehensible, ineffable. I can say no more . . . we are completely unable to measure by our intellect, or express it in words.

Likewise, when we experience contemplative union with God, it is so incredibly simple, yet it is far beyond our ability to communicate in words. Contemplative union with God is beyond human description. If we do try to describe it, it is like bursting a dam; we lose the treasure that we attempt to talk about.

In his writings, St. Bonaventure spoke of the simplicity yet utter infinity of the very being of God when he said,

> It is the very first and the very last, it is the origin and the final end of all things. Because it is eternal, and all present, surrounding and penetrating all duration, it is, as it were, both their center and their circumference. Because it is utterly simple and utterly great, it is wholly interior to all things and wholly exterior to them. "It is intelligible sphere, the center of which is everywhere, and the circumference of nowhere. Because it is supremely actual and immutable," while remaining unmoved, it imparts motion to all. Because it is wholly perfect and wholly immeasurable, it is interior to all things, yet not enclosed; exterior to all things, yet not all excluded; above all things, yet not aloof; below all things yet not their servant . . . Even though all things are many and pure being is but one, it is "all in all."

All of the previously mentioned aids in approaching simplicity, simple as they may be, are not really the simplest. They are only tools. The ultimate simplicity is not the tool, but the end for which the tool is created—God. This has been a key to Christian mystics through the centuries who have devoted their entire lives to the pursuit of God and total union with him. I believe all Christians should attempt to understand the role which contemplative prayer can play in their lives. We may not all be called to be monks. But we are all called at some level of our lives to contemplate the mystery of the incarnation, the life of Christ, and union with God.

Contemplative prayer is an extremely important concept—too important to treat in one part of one chapter. There have been many books written on contemplation, what it means and how to achieve it, but we cannot attempt to define these areas in this book. I can only say that it is important that each reader think about how contemplative prayer may be used to approach God in ways appropriate to his or her own lifestyle. I have written two books which cover contemplation more thoroughly: *The Fire of God*, and *The Lover and the Beloved* (both books, published by Crossroad/Continuum, New York, New York).

Let me close this section on contemplation by turning to the incarnation, which expresses beautifully the utter simplicity of God. We must ponder this staggering mystery in our hearts as Mary pondered it at Bethlehem when the shepherds visited the babe in the manger (Lk 2:19). It is a marvel beyond our comprehension.

For it is in the mystery of the incarnation that absolute simplicity and absolute infinity come together in a human being, in the person of Jesus Christ. St. Bonaventure said:

> In him, the first principle is united with the last to be created; God is united with man formed on the sixth day; eternity is united with time-bound humanity, with a man born of a virgin in the fullness of ages; utter simplicity is united with the most composite, pure action with supreme passion and death, absolute

perfection and immensity with lowliness, the supremely one and all inclusive with an individual composite man, distinct from every other; the man Jesus Christ.

St. Bonaventure continued:

> This consideration brings about perfect enlightening of the mind, when the mind beholds man made, as on the sixth day, in the image of God. Since, therefore, an image is an expressed likeness, when our mind contemplates, in Christ the Son of God, our own humanity so wonderfully exalted is so ineffably present in him; and when we thus behold in one and the same being both the first and the last, the highest and the lowest, the circumference and the center, the alpha and the omega, the caused and the cause, the creator and the created creature ... then our mind reaches a perfect object here as on the sixth day, it reaches with God the perfection of enlightenment.

St. Paul said in his letter to the Colossians that Jesus "is the image of the invisible God ... in him all the fullness was pleased to dwell" (Col 1:15, 19). In the Book of Hebrews it is written, "[He] is the refulgence of his glory, the very imprint of his being" (Heb 1:3). So God, in his divine simplicity, is manifested in the person of Jesus. This invisible reality is manifested in the visible reality, the person of Jesus Christ. God's simplicity is seen in the most complex of creatures—a human being—without losing its simplicity. This is mystery. This is paradox. It goes beyond logic and defies our mental faculties. It demands contemplation.

The pursuit of simplicity must incorporate a contemplative focus on God, the object of our faith. Simplicity requires that we seek to unite with our Creator in prayer and in contemplation.

MEDITATION AND CONTEMPLATION BRING US TO THE FOOT OF THE CROSS

As we contemplate the incarnation we are led inexorably to the cross of Jesus Christ—his supreme divine sacrifice for all humankind. Here we find we have gone full circle: meditation and prayer lead to contemplation, contemplation leads to the cross, the cross leads back to meditation and contemplation. Why is this cycle perpetuated? Mystery. When we meditate upon the cross we find that death and life are united, poverty and wealth are united, humility and glory are united. A total conclusion—and ultimate grasping of this meaning—is beyond us. We are, therefore, launched on a spiraling contemplative cycle which constantly strengthens our faith.

It is simple to state the reality of the cross—that Jesus died on it, that a Roman instrument of torture became a tool and a symbol in Christ's great redemptive act, that it stands today as a simple stark reminder of our Lord's sacrifice. But in reality it's beyond our ability to fully understand. Out of death comes forth life! The cross of Christ therefore becomes a great wonder—a point of meditation and contemplation for all serious Christians. It is a mystery and a paradox of the highest degree, and yet it is so simple.

St. Paul reminded Christ's followers that the message of the cross is complete absurdity to those who are headed for ruin, but for Christians it is the very power of God (1 Cor 1:18). "We proclaim Christ crucified," Paul said, "a stumbling block to Jews and foolishness to Gentiles"— a mystery containing the words of eternal life (1 Cor 1:23-24). It is a simple message and, again in Paul's own preaching he said, "When I came to you, brothers, proclaiming the mystery of God, I did not come with sublimity of words or of wisdom. For I resolved to know nothing while I was with you except Jesus Christ, and him crucified" (1 Cor 2:1-2).

As Christians we apply the crucifixion—the reality of the cross—to our own lives in ways which actually produce the fruit of the Holy Spirit. Those who belong to Jesus have crucified their flesh with its passions and desires. This crucifixion brings forth love, joy, peace, and the other fruits which are characteristic of our identity in Christ.

Of course, St. Francis is a supreme example of one who daily lived the message of the cross. He was a stigmatist— one who bore the mysterious marks of crucifixion on his hands and feet. Francis was ever on fire in his love for Jesus, the crucified Lord. For all Franciscans, the cross stands as the highest symbol of contemplation, the fullest expression of mysticism, and the greatest expression of full union with the simplicity of God. St. Bonaventure said of St. Francis, "The memory of Christ Jesus crucified was very present in the depths of his heart like a bundle of myrrh, and he longed to be transformed into him by the fire of love.''

The experience of St. Francis with the cross of Christ brings out the paradox of the cross. He was flooded with a mixture of joy and sorrow, the height and depth, the glory and humiliation, the comfort and the pain all at once. It all represented, however, one simple reality: his union with God through the cross of Jesus.

As Christians intent on coming into a fuller union with God through Christ, we must all bear the signs of Christ's crucifixion in our hearts. In other words, we must become stigmatists in an interior sense. Our internal stigmata will work its way outward in our lives as we feel, like Francis, the fiery arrow of love wounding our heart and soul, an experience we mystically share with the Redeemer.

All of this helps to explain why the cross became in Franciscan tradition, a simple, almost childlike devotional. The early Franciscans usually bowed before a crucifix when they entered or left a room which bore the image. They would even stop and acknowledge a cross when it appeared in nature—when the branches of a tree intersected to form the image, reproducing the remembrance of Christ's death and resurrection. Likewise, in our own lives, the cross should serve as a simple reminder of the great redemption we share in Christ. It should take us to an ever deeper, yet simpler walk of faith in our daily lives.

OUR NEED FOR DISCIPLINE AND AN ENVIRONMENT FOR PRAYER

In order to be united with God, the ultimate simplicity, we must create space and times in our lives which are conducive to consummating the union. Just as a husband and wife must set aside places and times in order to nurture a quality relationship, so must Christ and the Christian be assured of a proper environment and special occasions which help to forge the relationship of love.

Christians do this corporately by setting aside church buildings in which to worship and encounter God. Some people spend their entire lives studying the liturgical arts and church architecture in order to enhance the experience that the people of God have with their Creator in corporate worship. Historically, even the poorest areas of the world find Christians involved in their own cultural expressions of art, architecture, music, vestments, and sacramentals as they prepare themselves for corporate worship.

The same is true on a personal level for individuals who represent a microcosm of the church, since their own bodies are temples of the Holy Spirit, just as the church is the body of Christ. We, too, must set aside places and times that are undisturbed and free of distractions, so we can enjoy an optimum environment in which to pursue our love relationship with Jesus Christ.

As members of the Little Brothers and Sisters of Charity we follow our *Scripture Rule* which says, "Whenever you pray, go to your inner room, close the door, and pray to your Father in secret" (Mt 6:6). In the same Rule, we paraphrase from Mark 1, "Very early in the morning, while it is still dark, get up, leave the house and go to a solitary place and pray." Other similar Scriptures urge the community member to pray alone in the evening, to go to the hills and pray, to spend the night praying to God, and to withdraw frequently to lonely places to pray.

We know from Jesus' own example that he spent much

time in the mountains in solitary prayer (Lk 4:42; 5:16; 11:1). Before many of the major events of his life, he spent the night in communion with God. Often he would retire with three other brothers—usually Peter, James, and John—in order to experience God more intimately, yet within the context of community. This was certainly the case during the transfiguration. We also find that this same solitary yet communal prayer was used in the Garden of Gethsemane before his arrest, trial, and crucifixion. It was just such an example that prompted St. Francis of Assisi to establish the hermitage, not as a place of total isolation, but as a place of prayer in the midst of the brotherhood.

St. Francis knew the value of prayer discipline at appointed times and places. Eventually, Francis desired that his entire life would become a prayer. As Thomas of Celano wrote: "He made his whole time a holy leisure in which to inscribe wisdom in his heart, lest he would seem to fall back if he did not constantly advance . . . he always sought a hidden place where he could adapt not only his soul but also his members to God."

St. Francis sought particular environmental disciplines to aid his prayer. But Francis also knew that while the utmost of preparations could be taken in creating time and space for God, God is not programmable. Francis learned that he should be ready for unexpected visits from the Holy Spirit. Spontaneity, therefore, remained even in the midst of scheduled, disciplined prayer.

St. Francis and the early Franciscans have provided a model of community life which we follow here at the Little Portion. We attempt to strike a balance between solitude and community, contemplation and action. We live in individual hermitage cells clustered together around a common building and a common chapel. Individuals have quiet and privacy for personal prayer, meditation, and contemplation. But these individuals also come together for daily community prayer, worship, and daily meals—as well as community formation studies. We balance our prayer lives as contemplatives with apostolic action, including such work as maintenance of the property, office work, charitable pursuits, parish activities, and street ministry—just to name a few. Our community disciplines are structured in such a way that 50 percent of our time is spent in prayer, 50 percent in action.

Likewise, our Little Brothers and Little Sisters of Charity—who live in their own homes—are encouraged to create specific places and times of prayer, times of solitude and silence. Specific demands of the family and married life are taken into account so that appropriate relationships are maintained, even in the midst of the balance between prayer and action.

Statistics used by Marriage Encounter indicate that Christian couples who pray together have more successful marriage relationships, confirming the often-heard saying: "The family that prays together, stays together." I strongly urge couples and families to seriously consider establishing regular prayer disciplines in their lives for just this reason.

Finally, I would like to share a few thoughts on environmental asceticism and sensitivity in creating a setting for prayer by quoting from my latest book with

Crossroad/Continuum, *Hermitage*. As I say of both the monk and the monastery:

> A monk is a person who seeks God alone, that is all. A monk is a person on fire with love for God, one who has given all and separated himself from all, in order to know intense mystical union with the Creator of all. A monk should be like a man from another world. The things of this world should be totally tasteless to him. Yet, in this holy detachment, the monk should be the person who comes to truly experience the created world with a heightened awareness and heavenly appreciation that comes from knowing the Creator of the world. The monk is the one who turns only to heavenly realms, and so becomes effective on earth. The monk seeks to be a divine creature from another world, and so comes to bring the human reconciliation of Jesus to this world. The monk seeks to be a pilgrim and a stranger, and so is everywhere at home.
>
> Likewise, the monastery should be like a dwelling from another world. The allurements of the secular city should be totally absent in this city of God. Yet, the monastery should be a place of true artistic beauty and artistic balance, reflecting as a mirror on the earth the heavenly beauty and balance of the divine Artist. The monastery should be a place of keen environmental beauty and sensitivity, where the delicate and the fragile dimensions of all creation are fully experienced, appreciated, and favored, so as to lead the solitary community of monks to constant praise of God. Let the monastery be a place of audible and visual silence, so both

the small and great dynamic reality of the living word of God will be always sensitively received. Let it be a place of environmental asceticism, so as to foster a heightened awareness of the delicate aesthetic beauties of the created world. Yes, let the monastery be like a dwelling from another world, and it will increase the sensitivity to the created beauty of all the world and so help lead all creation to God.

Insofar as it is possible, all homes should reflect a greater or lesser degree of this reality of the monk and the monastery. Each person should seek God alone, like the monk, so that all other relationships will flow forth from our love relationship with God. In this regard, all Christians are called to be like monks. Likewise, each home should be like a monastery, so that all the buildings and cities of the earth will come to reflect the heavenly splendor and simplicity of God himself.

Practical Pointers on Developing a Life of Prayer and Meditation

1) Is inner simplicity possible without a life of prayer? Why not?

2) Why are disciplines and devotions of prayer and meditation—like the Rosary—so helpful? What prayer disciplines do you follow in your daily life?

3) Consider learning a new prayer devotion over the next couple of weeks that will help simplify and focus your life with God. Use it every day during your devotional time.

PART TWO

Exterior Simplicity: How We Can Simplify Our Lives

FOUR

Asceticism: A Key to Spiritual Freedom

L IKE OBEDIENCE, ASCETICISM IS a word most modern Americans would prefer not to hear. For many, the word
"asceticism" carries severe connotations of rigorous self-
denial and extreme conditions. For our purposes, however, asceticism will be defined primarily as self-
discipline. Frequently I will remind retreatants and
readers that the degree of asceticism or discipline appropriate for the individual will be determined by his or her
station in life. A celibate monk, a parish priest, a married
couple, and a university student will all vary substantially
in their need and in their ability to use ascetic measures in
their Christian lives. Each person must seek for him or
herself the degree of self-discipline that is appropriate and
helpful in a given situation. The key is to use such
discipline effectively to simplify our overly complicated
lives and center on Christ. Then asceticism can be a means
to genuine spiritual freedom.

DISCIPLINING THE TONGUE

Today we live in a world of ever-increasing sound levels: radios, TV's, vehicles, aircraft, and industrial sources of noise have pushed the decibel level into unhealthy ranges. And, it seems, at every turn we find that "talk is cheap." Many want to express themselves, but few are willing to truly listen. Fewer still are willing to voluntarily submit to the discipline of silence as part of their personal lifestyle.

In our community, the Little Brothers and Sisters of Charity have made covenant promises to live in substantial silence so that others might hear the Word of God. It is our desire that others might hear the voice of God as a mystery which bespeaks the paradox of the gospel. The more we enter into a voluntary discipline of silence, the more we believe the word of God will be heard.

It is like the pruning process spoken of earlier. Our words must be pruned back so that the word of God may be proclaimed. The less we speak, the more we communicate on a spiritual level. Proverbs 10:19 warns us of the dangers of a "multitude of words." Jesus himself urges simplicity in communication by teaching that our "yes" should really mean "yes" and our "no" should mean "no." Anything else, he said, is from the evil one. When our language is less than straightforward, duplicity easily enters in. I believe that Christians should communicate openly, directly, simply, and transparently.

Even our prayers should be simple and direct. In Luke 18, the conscience-stricken tax collector says simply, "O God, be merciful to me a sinner." Jesus said that this man "went home justified" (Lk 18:13-14). Consider the way St. Peter responds to Jesus when he sees the great miracle of the multiplication of fish, "Depart from me, Lord, for I am a sinful man" (Lk 5:8). This short prayer touched Jesus' heart and he responded, "Do not be afraid; from now on you will be catching men" (Lk 5:10). Peter's simple and contrite prayer led him to become one of the greatest preachers of the gospel and the leading apostle.

St. Paul said to the Colossians:

". . . you must put them all away: anger, fury, malice, slander, and obscene language. Stop lying to one another, since you have taken off the old self with its practices and have put on the new self, which is being renewed, for knowledge, in the image of its creator" (Col 3:8-10).

We are asked to amend our patterns of speech as part of our redemption. This is part of dying to the old self and rising a new person. As we become new creatures in Christ, we are to renew our speech so that our communication is proper and wholesome.

In his letter to the Ephesians, St. Paul wrote:

No foul language should come out of your mouths, but only such as is good for needed edification, that it may impart grace to those who hear. And do not grieve the holy Spirit of God, with which you were sealed for the day of redemption. All bitterness fury, anger, shouting, and reviling must be removed from you, along with all malice. . . . no obscenity or silly or suggestive talk, which is out of place, but instead, thanksgiving. (Eph 4:29-31; 5:4)

Here we see a direct connection between the working of the Holy Spirit and our words. St. Paul urges us to replace inappropriate talk with praise and thanksgiving.

"Eucharist" means "to give thanks." We are, therefore, to be a eucharistic people—a people of thanks and gratitude. There are important lessons to be learned in giving thanks, because expressing gratitude empowers the Spirit to move in our hearts and minds in a powerful way. Otherwise, our acts of self-discipline can produce a critical spirit instead of bringing us into spiritual freedom. Consider the following example from my own community experience.

In the Little Portion kitchen, we have mounted signs on our cupboards which read "bowls," "plates," "cups." Everything is labeled so that we may more efficiently function as a community in meal preparation and clean up. One day I went to get a bowl and found a plate in the wrong place! This annoyed me. But after placing the bowl in the appropriate place, I forgot about the incident. When it happened on three consecutive days, however, I began to feel anger rising up. Who is the culprit? I wondered. On the fourth day, I set a trap. While supposedly sipping coffee as I read a book, I observed community members going in and out of the kitchen. Sure enough, I spied the guilty party placing a bowl where the plates should be. Interestingly, I began to notice other things about this particular person which I found irritating.

Ultimately, I built an enormous case against the person in question. Through a series of inconsequential events, I actually reached the point where my relationship with the "guilty party" was severely threatened. I knew this was wrong, but how could I turn it around? I began by simply giving thanks. I thanked God that I shared a common faith in Jesus with this individual, shared ideals about charismatic Christian community, and other common goals. I then began to thank God for the great gifts and talents which this person possessed. Before long, I began to experience a change of heart. I found that not only did this person not annoy me, but a new love filled my heart for my fellow community member.

We may always have areas of disagreement with those around us. However, actively thanking God for one another will always bring out the overriding good which is in each person. A new perspective is brought into our lives which enhances love relationships in spite of the inevitable differences. An attitude of thanksgiving not only enhances our relationship with others, but it stirs up the Holy Spirit in our relationship with God.

Often we do not fully realize the constructive and destructive power in words. The Scriptures tell us that "Death and life are in the power of the tongue" (Prv 18:21). St. Paul stated to the Romans, "one believes with the heart and so is justified, and one confesses with the mouth and so is saved" (Rom 10:10). By virtue of our words, therefore, our eternal destiny is shaped! Sinning through words can kill. Righteousness in words can literally bring forth life.

It is in the twenty-eighth chapter of the Book of Sirach where we find Scripture's most devastating analysis of the power of the tongue:

Cursed be gossips and the double-tongued,
    for they destroy the peace of many.

A meddlesome tongue subverts many,
    and makes them refugees among the peoples;
It destroys walled cities,
    and overthrows powerful dynasties.
A meddlesome tongue can drive virtuous women
    from their homes
    and rob them of the fruit of their toil;
Whoever heeds it has no rest,
    nor can he dwell in peace.
A blow from a whip raises a welt,
    but a blow from the tongue smashes bones;
Many have fallen by the edge of the sword,
    but not as many as by the tongue. . . .
As you hedge round your vineyard with thorns,
    set barred doors over your mouth;
As you seal up your silver and gold,
    so balance and weigh your words.
Take care not to slip by your tongue . . .
    (Sir 28: 13-18, 24-26)

Sirach urges us to be consistent in our thoughts, steadfast in our words, swift to hear and slow to answer. He says that our tongue can be our downfall—we should say nothing harmful. "A kind mouth multiplies friends,/" he wrote, "and gracious lips prompt friendly greetings" (Sir 6:5).

Of gossip Sirach says:

. . . he who repeats an evil report has no sense.
Never repeat gossip
    and you will not be reviled. . . .

Let anything you hear die within you;
  be assured that it will not make you burst.
When a fool hears something, he is in labor,
  like a woman giving birth to a child.
Like an arrow lodged in a man's thigh
  is gossip in the breast of a fool. (Sir 19:5-6, 9-11)

We are to ignore gossip when it comes our way, and we are to admonish others to do the same. More practical counsel is nowhere to be found regarding slander and gossip. If simplicity is to be our aim, we must guard our tongue—and even our ears.

Thomas of Celano records that St. Francis detested gossipers. He saw their tongues as poisonous weapons. He believed that disaster would confront the Franciscan Order unless slanderers were checked. St. Francis saved some of his strongest words for those who criticized, detracted from others, slandered, and gossiped. This is one reason why silence was so important in Francis's rule for the hermitage, where the contemplative life was to be lived in an intense way. Of life lived in the hermitage of the Portiuncula (of the Little Portion) it was written:

Let them do as the old brothers did. This was already a holy place; they preserved its holiness by praying there continually night and day and by observing silence there constantly. And if they sometimes spoke after the time determined for the beginning of silence, it was always to converse about the glory of God and the salvation of souls with much uplifting fervor. If it so happened, and this was rare, that a brother engaged in a futile or inopportune conversation, he was immediately chided by another.

Similarly, holy silence permeated the contemplative life of St. Clare and her followers, the Poor Ladies of San Damiano, later called the Poor Clares. Thomas of Celano wrote: "They have so attained the singular grace of abstinence and silence that they need exert hardly any effort to check the movements of the flesh and to restrain their tongues. Some of them have become so unaccustomed to speak that when necessity demands that they speak, they can hardly remember how to form the words as they should . . ."

Here at the Little Portion hermitage, the Brothers and Sisters of Charity have adopted this asceticism in speech by observing holy silence, beginning at 10 P.M. and continuing until morning prayer at 7:30 A.M. Breakfast comes after morning prayer and communion in holy silence. We maintain silence until the noon meal at 12:15 P.M. daily. In the afternoon, work begins and we may speak freely to one another. We reconvene for evening prayer at 5:30 P.M. and then eat dinner. Silence begins again at 10 P.M. Our emphasis is that this silence not be a legalistic one, but rather a sacred and holy silence, a silence embraced out of love for God and love for neighbor. If we find that we must speak at a time of silence, we do so in a whisper and in extreme brevity.

We found that it was difficult to observe silence at first because all of us come out of a noisy, word-ridden world. Time is needed to withdraw from the cacophony. Now we find that silence is a wonderful experience, something we embrace out of love, not by law. Substantial times of silence have encouraged us to develop spirit-to-spirit and heart-to-heart communication without the use of words. We find that nonverbal communication begins to take place. Then when words are used, they are used far more effectively.

Our community has also established definite guidelines regarding gossip and slander. We simply follow the admonition of the Gospel of Matthew 18:15-17:

> "If your brother sins [against you], go and tell him his fault between you and him alone. If he listens to you, you have won over your brother. If he does not listen, take one or two others along with you, so that 'every fact may be established on the testimony of two or three witnesses.' If he refuses to listen to them, tell the church. If he refuses to listen even to the church, then treat him as you would a Gentile or a tax collector."

Here we find that appropriate channels of communication have been clearly established in the event that conflict should arise. At each stage, conversation is restricted to the appropriate parties for the purpose of restoring fellowship and allowing correction, not for punishment or damage.

Words are important! The appropriate use (and non-use) of words must be mastered by the serious Christian, particularly those seeking to simplify their lives. The Gospel of John, chapter 1 tells us that, "In the beginning was the Word, and the Word was with God, and the Word was God ... the Word became flesh and made his dwelling among us. . . " (vss. 1, 14). This concept of the incarnation of the Word of God arises from the Middle Eastern understanding of spoken words which are believed to represent the very soul of the human being. Therefore, words are not used lightly. They are not to be spoken cheaply or inappropriately. It could be said that when you speak, your soul goes forth and is shared with others. So, words are to be shared reverently and carefully. We would do well to reconsider and appropriate this ancient understanding of words so that our speech may be uplifting, edifying, direct, pure, honest—*simple*!

ASCETICISM IN USING POSSESSIONS: FREEDOM FROM THE THINGS OF THIS WORLD

Today we live in a lopsided world. The wealth and the resources of this planet are disproportionately distributed among the peoples who inhabit it. As Americans, we are 6 percent of the world's population, yet we consume 40 percent of the world's resources! Materialistic consumerism has become one of the great sins of western civilization. It is said that Mother Teresa, when asked which nation of the world was poorest, replied that it was America, referring to the great spiritual poverty and lack of love so evident in this nation. How ironic that our great material wealth has produced such poverty and sickness of the heart.

St. Francis of Assisi understood this irony very well when he stated: "If we had any possessions we should be forced to have arms to protect them, since possessions are a cause of disputes and strife, and in many ways we should be hindered from loving God and our neighbor. Therefore, in this life, we wish to have no temporal possessions."

In the modern world, we still find ourselves protecting our enormous national assets through force of arms. The nuclear arms we have today, however, are holocaust weapons of mass destruction.

An incredible thing happens in a modern economic system which buys and defends its possessions. I call it "the beast syndrome." It has to do with the very nature of capitalism. Capitalistic endeavors must either enlarge or decrease—it seems nearly impossible to simply maintain a healthy, moderate status quo. Of course, when faced with either of these options, the desire is to grow. As a business grows, more people, materials, marketing strategies, administration, and management are needed. A successful, simple business can become a monster which must be fed in order to keep the entire process moving forward. We create a beast, a system which requires more and more energy to operate. The simple exchange of a product for currency mushrooms into a complicated machine involving millions of lives and billions of dollars.

This can also happen in Christian ministries. When worthy Christian pursuits become dominated by worldly systems in order to "reach the world," the beast begins to take up residence within the ministry itself and the process of destruction begins. Soon Spirit-filled, Spirit-inspired gospel ministry can be subverted by the very system which sustains its growth and "effectiveness."

I have seen it happen on numerous occasions. A man or

woman receives a simple call from God to preach a particular message. This ministry begins, becomes popular, and people are drawn to it. Soon the minister requires a support system: an office, a telephone, a typewriter, support staff, computers and ever higher levels of technical assistance. The ministry enters a growth phase as the cycle continues. But often a subtle line is crossed. The support machinery is transformed into a beast when it shifts from an emphasis on propagating the gospel to one of sustaining and propagating itself.

In fact, some non-profit ministries and many profit-making, ministry-oriented retailers have become crassly materialistic and seemingly concerned only with the bottom line—all in a race to apply the latest and most advanced marketing strategies. God Almighty is replaced by the almighty dollar. Instead of ministries for God, they become ministries of the great whore of Babylon, using Jesus' name to legitimize worldly techniques and goals.

We know that God will judge and correct both the church when it falls into this trap and the harlot who lays it. This is why God's judgment will come fast and it will come hard. As the Scriptures say, ". . . In one hour your judgment has come . . . in one hour this great wealth has been ruined . . . In one hour she has been ruined" (Rv 18:10, 17, 19). Only those who serve the god of the dollar will be sad when judgment falls. Those who serve God will be happy because they will once again be free to move in the Spirit of God—to bring forth ministries which are truly born of the Spirit. They will once again proclaim the gospel without being hindered by the false god of the dollar whom so many serve in the name of Jesus Christ.

Sadly, I am having to deal with this reality in my own ministry. I am approached by those who desire that I create music or manuscripts based on saleability and potential profits, rather than on the message I feel God would have me share. Instead of hearing the question, "John, what do you believe the Lord is saying to you today?" I am hearing suggestions which go something like this: "John, if we just put the project together like this, our sales projections will be met." We must all be on guard not to fall into this trap! That includes artists, publishers, producers, middlemen, retailers, and buyers: sugar-coated Christianity is addicting both producer and consumer; both have become hooked. The choice is ours. We can withdraw through thoughtful discipline and prayer, or we can sink into ever deeper levels of destruction and deception.

Of course, all Christian ministries must deal with finances. Things must be done decently, in order, and with thoughtful, appropriate stewardship. Indeed, we are in the world, but we must not be of the world. As St. Paul stressed, money is not in itself evil. It is the love of money which is evil.

Yes, we must to some degree use the things of the world in order to reach the world. St. Paul wrote, "I have become all things to all, to save at least some" (1 Cor 9:22b). But there is an important lesson to learn: the beast must be kept in a cage, for once it is let out, it will consume, destroy, deceive, subvert, and try to nullify the true gospel of Jesus Christ.

The pruning process is constant—it never stops. It must be done yearly, quarterly, weekly, daily! We must reassess our own situation, not to the point of scrupulosity or bondage, but to the point of appropriate self-questioning. It is in the power of the Spirit that we must discern God's will and move forth in a balanced way to do his will, to preach his gospel, and to be witnesses in a lost world.

While I believe God will guide us through his Spirit on such matters, our own logic reveals the value of gospel poverty in attempting to spread our message. The less we have, the freer we are to give our gifts away. The more we are attached to the system, the more in danger we are of actually losing our ministry when that system falls. St Paul wrote, "I should like you to be free of anxieties . . . I am telling you this for your own benefit, not to impose a restraint upon you, but for the sake of propriety and adherence to the Lord without distraction" (1 Cor 7:32, 35). And remember the ringing words of Jesus himself: "For where your treasure is, there also will your heart be" (Lk 12:34).

If we lay up treasures on earth, even though they may be rationalized as stockpiles or fuel for ministry, the more we become fixed on earth and not on heaven. St Paul taught, ". . . seek what is above, where Christ is seated at the right hand of God. Think of what is above, not of what is on earth" (Col 3:1-2). St. Clare of Assisi said, "Leave the things of time for things of eternity. Chose the things of heaven over the things of the earth. Obtain the hundred-fold in place of the one and so possess a blessed and eternal life."

Practical Pointers on Asceticism

1) Do you tend to talk *too* much? Are you *too* attached to your possessions? Does silence stifle or enhance your communication with others? Do you think about *things* more than God and others?

2) What is "the beast syndrome"? How does it affect the way we live our lives in Western society? What can you do about it in your own life?

3) What is the logic of gospel poverty according to Jesus, St. Paul, and St. Francis? How can you respond to the call to gospel poverty, especially in the areas of speech and using your possessions? Be specific and honest with yourself. Ask for the advice of others.

4) After some time for discernment and prayer, decide to make a change in your lifestyle in one of these two areas. Humble yourself before God, be obedient to him, and seek him in daily prayer as you implement this change in your life.

FIVE

The Challenge of Countering Materialism with Gospel Poverty

G OSPEL POVERTY IS NOT only a helpful discipline in guarding our inner attitude of simplicity, it also must become an external reality in addressing one of the world's gravest problems—that of materialism. As noted, Americans represent only 6 percent of the world's population, yet we consume an enormous 40 percent of the world's resources. No matter how we try to rationalize this reality, it boils down to one thing in God's eyes: sin! Much of the rest of the world views it in the same way.

At least half the entire population of the earth goes to bed hungry each night. Billions go to bed too hot, too cold, without needed medical care, without proper employment, without education, without adequate shelter or clothing—without! By contrast, most Americans live in relative comfort and many in opulence. No nation, no people, has ever had it so good. How ironic that with technology advancing as it never has in human history, poverty overwhelms so many of the earth's people. There is an ever-widening gap between the rich and the poor. The sin is increasing.

Of course, we tend to rationalize the use and abuse of the many things we enjoy: our hairdryers, our microwave ovens, our VCRs, our expensive cars, and our recreational vehicles. Granted, none of these things in and of themselves is sinful. However, the unchecked accumulation of material things has become an evil which affects the entire planet. In the eyes of the rest of the world, our excuses for unbridled consumerism are simply beyond justification.

As Pope John Paul II wrote in his encyclical *On Social Concern*:

> A first negative observation to make is the persistent and often the widening of the gap between the areas of the so-called developed North and the developing South . . . One of the greatest injustices in the contemporary world consists precisely of this: that the ones who possess much are relatively few, and those who possess almost nothing are many. It is the injustice of the poor distribution of the goods and services originally intended for all. (No. 14)

Unfortunately, this is not the end of the scandal. American Christianity has actually propagated the sin of inequality rather than solving the problem through righteousness. Despite our television evangelists, our

Christian radio programs, and contemporary Christian music—despite our filled arenas and charismatic events—America has not repented. What is worse, much American Christianity has fallen for the satanic lie of materialism. We have attempted to find scriptural justification for materialism. We have done violence to the Scriptures by pulling them out of context to promote our wealthy lifestyles and economic greed. In actual fact, most American Christians live lives of incredible wealth compared to that lived by Jesus, the apostles, the early church believers, and the great saints of history.

The Vatican II document *The Church in the Modern World* states clearly:

> Many people, especially in economically advanced areas, seem to be dominated by economics; almost all of their personal and social lives are permeated with a kind of economic mentality. . . . In the midst of huge numbers deprived of the absolute necessities of life, there are some who live in riches and squander their wealth. . . . (No. 63)

We claim to have "found it." We call ourselves "born again." We have had a born-again "man in office." Our air waves are filled with the shallow messages of televangelists and radio preachers who press their public for even more donations—all in the name of Christian ministry. Our jetset contemporary Christian musicians fill airports, limousines, and first-class hotel suites across the nation. Sadly, many of our churches look more like expensive civic auditoriums than ornamented houses of prayer. Many of our pastors and preachers live in million dollar homes, take home hundreds of thousands of dollars in salaries, and move comfortably in the fast lane of our society.

We must come to understand that this kind of "Christianity" scandalizes humanity. Citizens of the Third World see through the empty facade of our lip service to Christ, calling us frauds and hypocrites in much the same way Jesus did in addressing the scribes and Pharisees. Sadly, Christians in many other parts of the world do not take American Christianity seriously as a result. If we are truly honest with ourselves, we must concede that much of their criticism is right on the mark.

But have we really come to understand the truly destructive effect of our materialism, not only upon the poor worldwide from whom we steal, but upon ourselves? Materialism and consumerism destroy not only those who are in want, but they destroy the very humanity and spirituality of those who are numbered among the wealthy. As Pope John Paul II wrote in his recent encyclical, *On Social Concern*:

This superdevelopment which consists of an excessive availability of every kind of material goods for the benefit of certain social groups, easily makes people slaves of "possessions" and of immediate gratification with no other horizon than the multiplication of continual replacement of the things already owned with others still better. This is the so-called civilization of "consumption" or "consumerism," which involves so much "throwing away" and "waste." An object already owned but not superseded by something better is discarded, with no thought of its possible lasting value in itself, nor of some other human being who is poorer.

All of us experience first-hand the sad effects of this blind submission to pure consumerism: In the first place a crass materialism, and at the same time a radical dissatisfaction, because one quickly learns—unless one is shielded from the flood of publicity and the ceaseless and tempting products—that the more one possesses the more one wants, while the deeper aspirations remain unsatisfied and perhaps even stifled. (No. 28)

In other words, through the continual building up of things in our lives, we become more thing-like. We actually become conformed to the image of that which fills our mind: things. We cease to be truly human. We stumble in our journey to reach our potential as true human beings. John Paul II concludes this point in his encyclical by saying:

This then is the picture: there are some people—the few who possess much—who do not really succeed in "being" because, through a reversal of the hierarchy of values, they are hindered by the cult of "having": and there are others—the many who have little or nothing— who do not succeed in realizing their basic human vocation because they are deprived of essential goods. (No. 28)

Thus, materialistic consumerism has a devastating negative effect on all involved—on the few who possess much and on the many who do not possess even their most basic needs. We would all do well to remember the timeless words of Ghandi: "Live simply so that others may simply live." We must differentiate between our wants and our needs, because it is our wants that are killing the needy. St. Francis of Assisi taught that when we take something we do not truly need, we are, in effect, stealing from the poor.

I want to be extremely careful in pointing out something: the sin of materialism, as such, does not consist of simply owning something. It is not my intention to inflict disproportionate guilt or scrupulosity about every possession we own. The pope says in his encyclical *On Social Concern*: "The evil does not consist of 'having' as such, but in possessing without regard for the quality or the ordered hierarchy of the goods one has. Quality and hierarchy arise from the subordination of goods and their availability to man's 'being' and his true vocation" (No. 28).

So what is the answer? Where do we draw the line? We must begin with the Scriptures which are the "canon" or "measuring stick" of the development of Christianity through the ages. I find that the Scriptures seem to demonstrate three main approaches to living out the gospel of poverty or simplicity. Not all people are in the same place in life. Likewise, not all people have the same call from God. Therefore, there may be various ways of living out gospel poverty—different angles from which to approach the challenge of simple living. None of the three ways are easy. On the contrary, they require commitment, faith, and perseverance.

THE IDEAL WAY OF THE MENDICANT

The first means of living out gospel povety is the most radical and is based on Matthew, chapters 10 and 19. In this approach, both individuals and groups are called to absolute poverty which involve no personal possessions whatsoever. This is the itinerant ideal in which the early apostles undertook—a radical simplicity that freed them to travel continually with no promise of a place to lay their heads, always ready to move on and spread the gospel of Jesus Christ. In Matthew 10:5-10 we read that Jesus sent his apostles on a mission, charging them not to visit pagan territory or Samaritan areas but to go to the lost sheep of the house of Israel. Jesus told them to cure the sick, raise the dead, heal the lepers, expel demons, and to share the gift that they had received. The apostles were asked not to take gold, silver, or copper, no bags, no changes of clothes, or even sandals—not even a walking staff! This was the earliest example of itinerant gospel ministry.

This kind of mendicant, apostolic poverty has a practical side, as brought out by Paul's first letter to the Corinthians where he speaks of the obligations and responsibilities of marriage, as opposed to the freedom of the celibate life. Paul urged that his readers should:

> ... be free of all anxieties. An unmarried man is anxious about the things of the Lord, how he may please the Lord. But a married man is anxious about the things of the world, how he may please his wife, and he is divided. An unmarried woman or a virgin is anxious about the things of the Lord, so that she may be holy in

both body and spirit. A married woman, on the other hand, is anxious about the things of this world, how she may please her husband. (1 Cor 7:32-34)

This was not a command from Paul, but his counsel. He said, "I am telling you this for your own benefit, not to impose a restraint on you, but for the sake of propriety and adherence to the Lord without distraction" (1 Cor 7:35).

There are two levels of gospel poverty which Jesus taught in Matthew 19 when he responded to the rich young ruler. You will recall that this young man—while he had kept all of the essential commandments—was unable to sell his possessions when challenged by Christ to do so. Jesus taught that our treasure would be in heaven. As the rich young man turned away, Jesus told his followers: ". . . it is easier for a camel to pass through the eye of a needle than for a one who is rich to enter the kingdom of God" (v. 24).

Not only does gospel poverty carry a practical dimension in that it frees one to follow Christ and to minister, but there is an internal sacrifice which—when made in faith—aligns us with the value Christ places on heavenly treasures, not earthly ones. In the same passage of Scripture (Mt 19:27-29), Peter turned to Jesus saying, "We have given up everything and followed you. What will there be for us?" Jesus responded that those who have followed him in giving up home, brothers and sisters, parents, wives, children, or property for his sake would receive many times as much and would inherit eternal life. Ironically, eternal wealth beyond our wildest imagination is available to those who will simply live a life of gospel poverty.

St. Anthony of the Desert, the father of monasticism, used these apostolic Scriptures of gospel poverty as the foundation stone of his life. Later in the history of the church, St. Francis of Assisi returned to Matthew 10 and 19 in founding the Franciscan Order, radically living out the gospel lifestyle Christ called for.

Likewise, our own community, the Brothers and Sisters of Charity, have as one of their foundational Scriptures, Matthew 10 and 19. In our itinerant ministry, we go out on foot, sometimes in pairs or sometimes in a larger group, taking no money. We have no idea what our destination will be. We do not know where we will eat or sleep. We live hand to mouth just like the apostles did and in much the same way as the early Franciscans did. Our only intention is to minister where Christ leads us. We find that we have always been taken care of by God. Jesus asked, "When I sent you forth without a money bag or a sack or sandals, were you in need of anything?" (Lk 22:35). The apostles replied that they had need of nothing.

This model goes against the "bigger is better" ideal we find prominent in our nation. We seem to have multi-million dollar ministries everywhere, yet conversion—true conversion—is hard to find. Many ministries seem to tolerate, and in some cases sponsor, greed and materialism rather than confronting them in a powerful and convincing way. We believe that the itinerant ministry is a credible, prophetic way to confront the materialistic values of our day. It is through the personal experience of sacrifice, through smallness and littleness, through true humility that a powerful message goes forth which challenges the values and institutions which need to be reformed by and comformed to the image of Christ. We have truly found that small is beautiful—and powerful! It is a call back to our gospel roots, to our Christian beginnings. We are attempting to bear witness to the authenticity of the gospels themselves, thereby drawing men and women to Jesus.

On a more practical level, we believe that we are preparing for the time when luxurious choices may no longer be options. Repeatedly throughout history, God has called countries to repent or suffer the devastating consequences. I believe our nation is in danger of falling under God's judgment. Indeed, it appears that in some ways, judgment has already begun. Prophecy after prophecy is foretelling a time when God will chasten the West, and prophets are crying out that it is time to prepare. If we refuse to divest ourselves of our materialism and consumerism, then perhaps God will do it for us.

Our itinerant ministry is an attempt to manifest just how God's Word can go forth, even when a large cash flow or a public relations campaign are impossible. All we really need in order to continue reaching out in Christ's name are our feet, our bodies, our voices, and our uplifted spirits. We have become poor that others may know the richness of God's eternal salvation and the wealth of his kingdom. Such a ministry is able to exist in any environment—whatever the economic, political, social, or cultural dimensions. We are free from the systems of the world to go forth in power and in simplicity.

Another prophetic dimension of an itinerant ministry is joy. We are able to demonstrate to the world that in spite of our poverty, we are filled with joy in Christ. Unfortunately, we live in an age when many feel deprived if they don't have a second car, a microwave oven, the latest video equipment, or a vacation home. These, of course, do not bring true joy. Indeed, they often bring stress and anxiety into our lives. Though we have nowhere to rest our heads, know not where we will eat, or what job we may do from day to day, we nevertheless go forth with a joy that transcends the so-called security of materialism. Indeed, this is a prophetic witness which is needed in our world, now more than ever.

I invite you to consider joining us in our itinerant ministry. Join our teams, join us in our prayer community, or—should you feel led by God—begin your own team or prayer community right where you are. Of course, you should seek the Lord and his discernment and will for your life. But you don't need to be highly trained or skilled. Remember: none of the apostles were trained in theology or schooled in universities! They were simple people called by Christ to go forth and minister the simplicity of the gospel. All you truly need is a converted life. Then go forth in such ministry under the Lord's guidance. In fact, all you need to do to evangelize is simply talk to your fellow human beings. Touch their lives in meaningful ways as God leads.

I see this more radical, mendicant way of living out gospel poverty as being like a lightning bolt. It is highly charged, sometimes very difficult, and is probably not a viable alternative for many Christians. This way of life is for the few who are called to it. It is much like lightning, in my view, because this kind of apostolate goes forth in explosive power shedding light and transmitting energy at a very high level. Historically, those who take up this way of life in the church witness somewhere for a brief period of time and then are gone. It is highly prophetic, and it is through the dedicated example of a few people that this kind of ministry bears a special kind of powerful witness in our world.

THE MORE APPROACHABLE MONASTIC WAY: A CALL TO COMMUNITY LIFE

A second way of living out gospel poverty is based on the Scriptures found in Acts 2 and 4. It is the monastic or communal way of poverty. At about the same time that St. Anthony of the Desert established his eremitical way of life based on Matthew 10 and 19, St. Pachomius also lived in the deserts of Egypt. He did not live as a hermit or wander forth to preach from time to time. He simply gathered a group of men about him to live a communal way of life. He then developed a centralized government to help guide the many thousands who joined together in monasteries to live out the Scriptures in Acts which read:

> They devoted themselves to the teaching of the apostles and to the communal life, to the breaking of the bread and to the prayers. Awe came upon everyone, and many wonders and signs were done through the apostles. All who believed were together and had

all things in common; they would sell their possessions and divide them among all according to each one's need. (Acts 2:42-45)

The Scriptures further describe this communal life:

The community of believers was of one heart and mind, and no one claimed that any of his possessions was his own, but they had everything in common. . . . There was no needy person among them, for those who owned property or houses would sell them, bring the proceeds of the sale, and put them at the feet of the apostles, and they were distributed to each according to need. (Acts 4:32, 34-35)

In this early church community, the more radical, apostolic ideal was lived out in a more approachable, liveable way in the city of Jerusalem. They were not called to wander across the face of the earth, but called to live gospel poverty according to the teaching of Jesus right where they lived. They took the poverty ideal and began to apply it to a more stable way of community life, enabling larger numbers of people to express their common faith in this way.

St. Pachomius reflected these values in his own community and further adaptations were made by St. Basil in the East and St. Benedict in the West. Ultimately, this form of monasticism became so widespread that the more radical eremitical form founded by St. Anthony began to disappear.

Today this strict communal ownership alluded to in

Acts 2 and 4 is seen in many intentional covenant communities where men and women—even families—live under one roof or in one general area. This way of life is then not only for celibate men or women but may be lived out by broader segments of the church.

After St. Francis reintroduced the gospel-poverty model from Matthew 10 and 19 into the monastic tradition, these two ideals (the mendicant and communal) did not go forth as separate streams, but became part of one large river of religious life flowing out into Christian history. Thus, in the home base of a religious community, Christians would often hold all things in common, patterned after Acts 2 and 4. Then they would proceed forth periodically in evangelistic and itinerant ministry teams where they would literally live out the Matthew 10 and 19 model.

Here at the Little Portion hermitage we have combined these two in the following way: we live the stable way of life based on Acts 2 and 4 in our hermitage, but we venture out from this hermitage into itinerant ministries as mentioned earlier. Therefore, we don't exclusively live either the stable life of a monastery or the itinerant life on the road. We alternate back and forth between the two.

Admittedly, neither of these two examples are commonly applied to the life of the average Christian who nevertheless wants to undertake radical simplicity. Few people are able to undertake the itinerant life, nor are many called to a strict community. Most Christians live in their own homes. They hold jobs. They have families to raise and bills to pay. Consequently, they have to deal with bank accounts, private possessions, and other practical responsibilities. I believe that for many Christians the third way of gospel poverty can be the highest challenge.

THE DOMESTIC WAY: OPEN TO
THE MANY, INCLUDING FAMILIES

The third way of gospel poverty is alluded to in Paul's second letter to the Corinthians where he says:

> "...I am giving counsel on this matter...not that others should have relief while you are burdened, but that as a matter of equality your surplus at the present time should supply their needs, so that their surplus may also supply your needs, that there may be equality" (2 Cor 8:10, 13-14).

In this passage, we find that Paul has taken the ideal life of Jesus and the apostles, the more approachable, yet still prophetic life of the first church in Jerusalem, and then applied them to the very real cultural circumstances which he has encountered in Corinth. This is admittedly a moderate pastoral approach. He says at the beginning of this discourse, "...you know the gracious act of our Lord Jesus Christ, that for your sake he became poor although he was rich, so that by his poverty you might become rich" (2 Cor 8:9). He admits that Jesus' way is to become destitute and poor, yet he seems to modify this ideal so it might be practically lived out by the many. Matthew 10 and 19 is an ideal way; it is highly prophetic! Acts 2 and 4 is also highly prophetic, and it is approachable for those so called. Second Corinthians 8 is practical for the many, liveable in the secular world, and still prophetic.

St. Paul's admonition to the Church that there be equality cannot be ignored. We must ask ourselves the question: Is there truly equality between the First World and the Third World? The answer is an obvious no. In fact, we know that the gap is actually widening. But let's look closer to home. Is there equality between the rich, suburban parishes of our American cities and the impoverished inner city parishes? The answer, again, is no. Finally, within our parishes, is there equality between those who are wealthy and those who are poor? Sadly, the answer is no. Even within our own churches, there is a scandalous chasm that exists between the wealthy elite and the desperately poor in far too many cases.

We must conclude, therefore, that the most minimum requirement of gospel poverty found in the New Testament is not being met, particularly in our own country where we are falling far short of even the most lenient gospel mandate. This is a scandal to humanity. Even though we have the right to personal possessions, we must approach all of our possessions as though we have none. Ultimately, they belong to God. In the Vatican II document, *The Constitution on the Church in the Modern World,* we are taught: "God destined the earth and all it contains for all men and all peoples so that all created things would be shared fairly by all mankind under the guidance of justice tempered by mercy" (No. 69).

The church does teach that private property is legitimate. However, it qualifies this concept by stating, "Therefore every man has the right to possess a sufficient amount of the earth's goods for himself and his family.

This has been the opinion of the Fathers and Doctors of the Church, who taught that men are bound to come to the aid of the poor and to do so not merely out of their superfluous goods" (*The Church in the Modern World*, No. 69). We see that the fathers and the doctors of the church held this view, teaching that men and women are obligated to come to the relief of the poor and to do so not merely out of their excess goods. The church teaches that ownership of private property implies social responsibility. If this responsibility is ignored, ownership of property often becomes an occasion of greed and disorder:

> By it's nature private property has a social dimension which is based on the law of common distinction of earthly goods. Whenever the social aspect is forgotten, ownership can often become the source of greed and serious disorder, so that its opponents easily find a pretext for calling the right itself into question. (No. 71)

All people—whether married, single, parents, or children—have the responsibility to embrace gospel poverty just as radically on an interior level as those who live it out in the itinerant ideal of Matthew 10 and 19. They should be just as committed as the monastic expressions of Acts 2 and 4. All that really differs is the external expression of poverty which everyone is not called to embrace. Jesus stated clearly in Luke 14:33, ". . . everyone of you who does not renounce all his possessions cannot be my disciple." This is an interior, minimum requirement of the gospel.

But you may be thinking, how can this be done? How can I respond to this call in my everyday life, in my neighborhood, in my parish? I cannot answer that question for you. Seek God, and he will show you.

I am reminded of a doctor in Canada who was extremely wealthy and lived a luxurious lifestyle. The Holy Spirit began to convict him and his wife in such a way that they felt called to become very poor. Today they are radically involved with Christ's call to gospel poverty. They accept only as much money as they need for the immediate week ahead. Everything else goes to the poor. Instead of a Cadillac or a Mercedes-Benz, they drive a Volkswagen. They gave up their exclusive suburban home for an inner-city home that has become a shelter to children in need. Indeed, this is a relatively rare expression of self-sacrifice, service, and love. But this couple stands as a model of faith in action, motivated by a commitment to gospel poverty.

All three ways of embracing gospel poverty are legitimate to those so called. In communities such as our own, all three are in operation. We have itinerant ministry teams, we have the monastic prayer model, and we incorporate families and volunteers into the structure of our lives. We are continuing to work out our community witness, and we encourage others to seriously consider the call of the gospel in their lives: to address the grave problem of materialism by embracing a life of gospel poverty.

Practical Pointers on How to Counter Materialism with Gospel Poverty

1) What happens when the few possess much and the many possess relatively little? Cite some examples in

the world today. What is the church's teaching on how we as Christians should approach such an imbalance?

2) What are the three scriptural models of gospel poverty? Which model do you think is most practical for your daily life? Why?

3) Consider one simple, practical way you can live out the call to gospel poverty, following one of the three models. Seek God in prayer and seek the counsel of other Christians you trust before you make a decision about changing your lifestyle. Follow through on your decision in a spirit of humility, in obedience to the Lord, and in daily prayer.

SIX

Simplicity of Life on Planet Earth: Our Response to a Growing Threat

T HE DISPROPORTIONATE DISTRIBUTION of the world's wealth, fueled by crass materialism, has further upset the balance of our planet, a balance that was seriously disturbed when our first parents sinned. Social structures, governments, economic systems, and the earth's delicate environmental balance have all been affected negatively by a minority whose greed and lust for power threatens our very existence. And each of us has contributed to the problem by our own personal sins, many times those of apathy and indifference in the face of serious institutional wrongs. "Spaceship earth" and its inhabitants are indeed in danger.

Amazingly, it is in the past fifty years—a relatively brief moment in the history of humankind—that so many ominous developments have taken place. And these are developments which must be addressed to avert international chaos. A huge demographic shift has taken place in the United States, for instance, since the turn of the century. I am told by experts that approximately one out of twenty-four families lived in cities while the rest farmed at that time. By the end of the Second World War, the figures had reversed themselves to only one out of twenty-five families living on a farm. Now we find that only two out of a hundred or one out of fifty American families are involved in agriculture. I believe this has vast ramifications for our society, our economic system, our environment, and even the ecology of the entire planet.

Our basic needs consist of food, clothing, and shelter. Of these three, food is obviously the most important to our survival. When a majority of society's families are agriculturally based, nutritional needs are being met by the majority. This keeps the entire population of a country very much in touch with, and in control of, its basic needs. It also enables each local area of a nation to produce what it needs for itself through a diversified agricultural program. In such a situation, trade and professional services are more localized and the structure of community more firmly established. At one time, this was the norm in our nation.

But a dramatic shift has taken place, and America has become urbanized in the 1900s. Industrial progress and increased wealth, centered in urban environments, has produced a population shift with heavy economic and social consequences.

Recently our itinerant ministry team had the opportunity to walk on foot through North Little Rock, Arkansas. It's amazing how much you see when you're on foot! We were amazed at the kind of businesses which lined the streets of this city. It seemed to us that nine out of ten were really unnecessary, only catering toward the wants and whims of American consumers, rather than meeting real, substantial needs. We have become a society which is oriented toward wants, thereby depriving others of real needs. Most of the industry and retailing we observed seemed to be superficially commercial, promoting and appealing to an artificial way of life. This produces a population which is out of touch with its true needs as its citizens are bombarded by products and marketing strategies which remove them farther and farther from reality.

Such an imbalanced system will surely lead to a fall if left unchecked. When a system like this appeals to wants rather than real needs, the system itself is in danger of rising and falling with the whims, rather than the constant needs, of its people. It is doomed to fail.

In fact, this seems to be, in part, what happened to the Roman empire. As the citizens in Rome grew more accustomed to luxury and less in control of basic food production, a formerly powerful civilization began to experience cracks in its culture—and ultimately in its way of life. The Romans were deceived and lulled into a false sense of security; they became top-heavy. Finally, they fell.

Of course, this analysis is not meant to imply that the Roman decline was simply a product of top-heavy economic and agricultural systems. The root problem was a moral one. I feel that America is dangerously close to the same situation today in both regards. We have become a superfluous, immoral society producing artificial products, locked in a cycle of consumerism and glitz which is affecting all of humankind through the exporting of American values and the exploitation of Third World countries.

How has the demographic shift affected the environment and health? With far fewer families tilling the soil, much more land is farmed per family. The old days of diversified agricultural programs have given way to new farming techniques which are based on vast tracts of farmland given to specialized, single crops. In order to control production on gigantic farms, hi-tech equipment, chemical fertilizers, herbicides, and pesticides are used in enormous quantities. Personal attention to an acre of land has given way to mechanized concentration on thousands of acres. Now when a family sits down to eat dinner, it is consuming food which comes not from a few miles away, but from literally thousands of miles away. You might say that we go thousands of miles to eat dinner every night!

Our very health is at stake as agrobusiness incorporates questionable techniques and substances in food production from livestock to grain. Only in recent years have we begun to discover just how important our food chain is to our physical well-being, and how it has been disrupted and threatened by the techniques of agrobusiness.

The environment has also been affected by industrial pollution and residential waste. Soil, rivers, and lakes are polluted, some to a degree beyond our ability to clean up. Consider the Exxon oil spill in early 1989 which proved impossible to contain and has had disastrous affects on the surrounding ecosystems in Valdez, Alaska. Many of the chemicals we use and the products we demand have created danger to the earth's ozone layer which protects us from ultraviolet rays of the sun—rays which already seem to be giving rise to frighteningly new levels of skin cancer, even among young people. According to the theories of some scientists, the gradual warming of the atmosphere through the greenhouse effect could carry with it enormous consequences. If left unchecked, it may result in worldwide catastrophes such as dramatic climatic changes.

We have gorged ourselves through policies of immediate gratification at the expense of long-range well-being. We are in deep trouble. Unless we simplify our lifestyles, humankind and the environment may not survive the growing crisis. It seems, however, that Americans will not simplify their lives on their own. As a nation, we're locked into systems and habits which addict us, lusting after things we don't need, blind to the judgment we are bringing on ourselves. It is because of this that I believe the system will fall. I do not want to be alarmist, but the handwriting seems to be on the wall. Unless a change takes place, painful as it may be to many, the results may prove incalculable for our nation.

I am not attempting to preach gloom and doom. I'm trying to motivate us in love to reverse the dangerous trends just highlighted. If everything we have come to rely on in our society disintegrates, if God's judgment comes, it is because he loves us. It is not out of wrath that God will allow these things to take place. Rather, it will be a chastisement from our loving Father. The Scripture says "Endure your trials as 'discipline'; God treats you as sons.

For what 'son' is there whom his father does not giscipline?" (Heb 12:7).

In 1 Timothy 6:8, St. Paul addresses Timothy, saying, "If we have food and clothing, we shall be content with that." Sirach 29:21 states, "Life's prime needs are water, bread, and clothing, /a house, too, for decent privacy." Based upon these two Scriptures, I would like to look at the three basic areas of human need and see how we might simplify our lives in these areas. They are food, clothing, and shelter.

HOW WE CAN SIMPLIFY OUR DIET

One of the best places to begin looking for Scriptures on the consumption of food is in the Old Testament Wisdom literature, specifically in the Book of Sirach. Sirach teaches in 37:26-30:

> My son, while you are well, govern your appetite
>   so that you allow it not what is bad for you;
> For not every food is good for everyone,
>   nor is everything suited to every taste.
> Be not drawn after every enjoyment,
>   neither become a glutton for choice foods,
> For sickness comes with overeating,
>   and gluttony brings on biliousness.
> Through lack of self-control many have died,
>   but the abstemious man prolongs his life.

The practical effects of simplicity in food are brought out further in Sirach 31:12, 19-20, 22:

> If you are dining with a great man,
>   bring not a greedy gullet to his table,

Nor cry out, "How much food there is here!"
    Remember that gluttony is evil . . .
Does not a little suffice for a well-bred man?
    When he lies down, it is without discomfort.
Distress and anguish and loss of sleep,
    and restless tossing for the glutton!
Moderate eating ensures sound slumber
    and a clear mind next day on rising. . . .
In whatever you do, be moderate,
    and no sickness will befall you.

And consider the effects of overeating on the pocket-book, of which we read in Sirach 18:30-33; 19:1:

Go not after your lusts,
    but keep your desires in check.
If you satisfy your lustful appetites
    they will make you the sport of your enemies.
Have no joy in the pleasures of a moment
    which bring on poverty redoubled;
Become not a glutton and a winebibber
    with nothing in your purse. . . .
He who does so grows no richer;
    he who wastes the little he has will be stripped bare.

And what of the spirituality exhibited in table etiquette itself? Much of a person's inner spirit can be seen in small external actions and much of a person's inner spirit can be directed by exterior discipline. Sirach says in 31:13-18; 32:1-2:

No creature is greedier than the eye:
    therefore, it weeps for any cause.

Recognize that your neighbor feels as you do,
   and keep in mind your own dislikes:
Toward what he eyes, do not put out a hand;
   nor reach when he does for the same dish.
Behave at table like a favored guest,
   and be not greedy, lest you be despised.
Be the first to stop, as befits good manners;
   gorge not yourself, lest you give offense.
If there are many with you at table,
   be not the first to reach out your hand. . . .
If you are chosen to preside at dinner, be not puffed up,
   but with the guests be as one of themselves;
Take care of them first before you sit down;
   when you have fulfilled your duty,
   then take your place,
To share in their joy
   and win praise for your hospitality.

Sirach gives very good advice on food and manners!

In Romans 14:17, St. Paul addressed the Romans: ". . . the kingdom of God is not a matter of food and drink, but of righteousness, peace, and joy in the holy Spirit." This, of course, is the kind of freedom and joy we notice in the life of Jesus and his apostles—they did not live in monasteries, nor did they live as monks. They were wandering, itinerant preachers. They relied heavily on the hospitality of others, for as the Scriptures say they had "nowhere to rest their heads."

In Luke 10:7-9 Jesus spoke to the seventy-two when he sent them out on mission, saying, "Stay in the same house and eat and drink what is offered to you, for the laborer deserves his payment. . . . Whatever town you enter and they welcome you, eat what is set before you, cure the sick in it . . ." This meant that scrupulous attention to the law regarding dietary norms had to go; freedom had to enter. As the church branched out beyond the people of Israel, early Christians encountered "unclean food" and were faced with the dilemma of whether to eat it or not. It is interesting to see in Acts 10:9-15 how Peter's vision of unclean animals, which he was commanded to eat, altered his rigid Judaic interpretation of the law. Peter received a new freedom which allowed missionary expansion among the gentiles of the world.

On the other hand, Jesus also spoke of a healthy asceticism regarding food and drink. Specifically, this took the form of fasting. Remember that Jesus entered his public ministry with a time of solitude, silence, and forty days of fasting in the desert. Matthew 4:1-2 records that "Then Jesus was led by the Spirit into the desert to be tempted by the devil. He fasted for forty days and forty nights, and afterwards he was hungry." Through prayer and fasting, Jesus overcame the severest of tests.

Jesus also taught his followers how to fast. In his Sermon on the Mount, Matthew 6:16-18, he said,

"When you fast, do not look gloomy like the hypocrites. They neglect their appearance, so that they may appear to others to be fasting. Amen, I say to you, they have received their reward. But when you fast, anoint your head and wash your face, so that you may not

appear to be fasting, except to your Father who is
hidden. And your Father who sees what is hidden will
repay you.''

The Christian is to fast with a whole new spirit, a spirit of
joy, and a spirit of freedom. Yes, we will have our tests and
we will have our temptations. We will find ourselves, at
times, in the desert. It is within these tribulations that
prayer and fasting will bring us to new levels of joy and
fulfillment in the Spirit.

Here at the Little Portion hermitage, we have embraced
the scriptural admonitions regarding fasting and simplification of food in ways we never thought possible! We
grow our own vegetables, we have chickens and goats
which provide eggs, meat, and milk. And we derive
protein from beans and rice. As a result we have cut our
average meal to a cost of less than fifty cents per person!

We have found, to our amazement, that a great many
grocery stores and restaurants discard food which is
healthy and edible. How tragic that in an age when thousands are dying of starvation at any given minute, tons of
perfectly good food are being wasted. For this reason, we
have started a local food bank in which volunteers collect
food (perfectly healthy) destined for the dumpster and
give it to the poor.

Fasting is also an important part of our community life.
We fast on bread and water twice a week. We have found
this to be a wonderful discipline which allows us to
empathize directly with the poor and teaches us the
difference between our wants and our needs.

Fasting can be a powerful tool in the life of a Christian. When used appropriately, it is good for the body, cleansing it of impurities, and enhancing the powers of the mind. Fasting can break our addiction to unhealthy habits such as fat, sugar, alcohol, caffeine.

There are many ways in which to fast. A person may fast by abstaining from any one thing: water, solid foods, even sleep. A person may also choose to abstain from all food and water for a day or a combination over a period of days. One form of fasting may be to simply cut out something we would like each day or at each meal. Here at the Little Portion, for example, we have desserts only on Sunday. We also attempt to be careful about additives, seasonings, or flavorings. We have tasty, yet simple meals, eliminating additives, artificial seasonings, or flavorings.

While it is good to fast according to liturgical cycles such Lent or Advent, religious disciplines should not be the only factor involved. We should be sensitive to the moving of the Spirit to lead us beyond ritual into special times of fasting. St. Francis, for example, recognized this combination of gospel freedom and flexibility. He practiced it with true spiritual discipline and fervor. St. Bonaventure reported that St. Francis, "On his missionary journeys, in preaching the gospel took whatever food was put before him by those who gave him hospitality. But when he returned home, he kept strictly to the rule of fasting. He was hard on himself but accommodating toward his neighbor. In this way he obeyed Christ's gospel in everything and did people as much good by eating as by fasting." Again, this illustrates the balance which we must strike between law and freedom, love and discipline.

I highly recommend the popular and helpful book *God's Chosen Fast* by Arthur Wallis, which may be ordered in Christian bookstores. The book is a practical guide to health issues in fasting and makes some excellent spiritual points, identifying God's purposes for fasting. One caution is in order, though: always seek medical advice before deciding to pursue serious fasting.

HOW WE CAN SIMPLIFY OUR WARDROBE

In 1974 the Simple Living Project, an outgrowth of the American Friends Service Committee in San Francisco, put out a manual on simple living entitled *Taking Charge*. There was an interesting commentary within this manual on clothing: "The American public spends 60 billion dollars a year on clothes, enough, it would seem, to drape the earth, yet for all that money American clothes are often uncomfortable, unuseful, unhealthy, and don't express our unique personalities." We can certainly conclude that since 1974 things have gotten worse. We could probably drape the earth many times over. Yet most of the world is poorly clothed and billions go hungry.

What is particularly disturbing about the American approach to clothing is the disproportionate focus on style and fashion. Fads come and go, and those who dictate them use marketing techniques which make us feel less "with it" or somehow less human unless we align ourselves with the latest expressions in fashion and design. This leads to cycles of buying and discarding which become enormously wasteful. Many of the clothes we wear are simply not suited for our everyday lives—we get caught up in wearing fashionable clothes which are impractical and inefficient.

This stands in stark contrast to Jesus' teaching when he sent the apostles forth on their mission: "Take nothing for the journey, neither walking stick, nor sack, nor food, nor money, and let no one take a second tunic" (Lk 9:3-4). The general principle found in this Scripture and similar Scriptures found in Mark 6 and Matthew 10 is to travel light and take only what is truly needed.

When our community goes out on itinerant missions, we discover the lesson of Christ's teaching. When I carry one extra book, one extra pair of socks, anything extra, enough weight is added so that after a day of trekking for miles in the hot sun, every ounce feels like a pound, every pound like ten pounds! The message of simplicity is driven home with greater force. I submit that large wardrobes are definitely a reflection of our wants rather than our needs. We have become motivated by the consumerist ideals of our culture rather than the life-giving simplicity of the kingdom of God.

But, again, let's be sure we keep the right balance! Yes, the apostles were sent forth "stripped for action" and early church saints, as well as Old Testament prophets, were noted for their ascetic lifestyles and their simple dress, but it is also important to note that there is a time and place for special clothing considerations and possessions. Remember when Paul said to Timothy in 2 Timothy 4:13 that he needed the cloak he left in Troas and he wanted his books and parchments returned to him. Obviously, we must consider which possessions and which clothing to maintain and which to avoid as worldly entrapments.

Jesus is interested in our motives. Consider, for example, religious garb. In Matthew 23:5 Jesus charged the scribes and Pharisees with widening their garments and wearing huge tassels. Obviously, he saw this as an expression of pride and religious power. It was not that the religious garments themselves were in question, but particular modifications represented interior attitudes.

Today's religious habits are a symbolic expression of the desire for gospel simplicity. Brown sackcloth and sheepskins have given way to habits in the monastic tradition such as may be seen on nuns, monks, Franciscan priests, and other religious brothers and sisters. While the habits may vary according to work needs, climate, or specific identification with religious orders, they do communicate a kind of simplicity and rejection of the world's fashions, fads, and temporal concerns. As St. Ephraim stated, "Reflect on the habit you wear and note the difference between it and the clothing of the world; diligently take into account what the religious garb signifies. It denotes abandonment of things worldly and carries with it an awareness of dedication to spiritual works."

Innocent III in his document *The Mysteries of the Sacred Altar,* further states that the religious habit is not merely an empty symbol but one which should be worn with integrity: "Let the bishop and the priest each examine diligently and pay studious attention to make certain that he does not bear the sign without bearing also that which it signified; that he does not wear the garb without the virtue, lest he be like the whitened sepulchre outwardly, but inwardly filled with all uncleanliness." St. Bernard also issued a similar warning and condemned those who had begun to wear the habit as a sign of pride instead of a mark of humility. Thus it remains important that human motives be pondered and tested.

St. Francis of Assisi clearly reformed the idea of a habit. He simply wore sackcloth and a rope around the waist. Though his garments changed from time to time, depending on the weather or upon his circumstances, he always dressed simply, even to the point of donning the rags of a beggar in exchange for his own habit, as actually happened on at least one occasion. Francis considered the needs of his neighbor more important than his own—a personal, spiritual value which is exactly the reverse of the "me generation" of the 1980s and 1990s in the West.

Here at the Little Portion hermitage, we have opted to retain the traditional monastic habit while still making provision for an adapted habit, depending on the particular commitment which has been made to the community. We try to avoid the "wardrobe syndrome," so we usually wear habits or modified habits as well as work-clothes when they are called for. In this way, our clothing needs are radically reduced. This means there is less time and money tied up in wardrobe concerns.

My own experience shows that the habit makes my life extremely flexible! I no longer have to make a decision as to what clothes to wear in the morning—the decision is already made for me. My habit is widely accepted, whether I'm walking through the village of a Third World country, singing from a stage in a stadium, appearing on television, or even meeting with religious and political leaders. Everywhere my habit is accepted as "formal" and "informal" wear! The habit also stands for the spiritual values that we believe are so desperately needed in our world. It constantly reminds others, and ourselves, of the commitment we have made to Christ and to our community. It is a silent witness in a noisy world. It is a simple garment in a complex, showy society.

For those who are living in the world, but desire not to be of the world, I would make a few suggestions. Dress simply in whatever context you find yourself. If you have a job, buy a couple of changes of clothes to suit the job. This might mean a couple of changes of work clothes or uniforms for blue-collar workers. Or it might mean a couple of business suits for the office worker. Also for off hours you way want a couple of changes of clothes for leisure, a change for recreation, and something for special social occasions. The important thing to remember is that your clothing be functional, tasteful, and appropriate to the situation.

Modesty is a consideration in any one of the above contexts. One of the scandals of the American fashion industry is the pervasive focus on sexuality. Women have been told through a constant bombardment of advertising and marketing techniques that they must look sexy, that the way they dress should appeal to men. Of course, the same is becoming true of sales pitches which are made to men. As Christians we should avoid falling into this trap. Sometimes it's very subtle, other times it's extremely obvious. At all times we must thoughtfully consider the choices we are making, and the affect those choices have on others around us.

There are also justice issues which should be contemplated when purchasing any kind of product, including clothes, which is imported from other countries. It is very common for clothing industries to produce garments in other countries where labor is cheap and working conditions inhumane. Once while visiting Haiti, I came upon a clothing factory located in the midst of abject poverty. Initially, I thought it was a positive development because jobs were being provided for people in a city where so many were out of work. On closer examination, however, I saw that the conditions of this particular plant were absolutely and utterly appalling. It was like a sweathouse!

The kinds of working conditions I saw were outlawed in the United States before the turn of the century. Extremely poor people are many times paid shamefully low wages to work long hours in many Third World factories of American-based corporations. This travesty is perpetuated because relatively wealthy Americans continue to buy products, and in this case, clothing produced in such factories.

This is a form of economic exploitation which must be addressed by the serious Christian. It gives us all the more reason to simplify our purchasing habits, especially when we buy our garments. We may find that we have unwittingly contributed toward social injustice by spending our dollars in support of Third World factories that oppress their workers in the production of consumer goods for Americans. Of course, this is a complex economic problem, and many factories operating outside the United States are run humanely. The point is to use discernment in making our purchases, so we don't unknowingly contribute to social injustice.

Remember the words of Jesus in Luke 12:27-28: he told us we could learn from the lilies of the field. They do not spin, they do not weave, but they are—Jesus said—arrayed with much greater splendor than even King Solomon in all of his wealth. How much more is he concerned with us! I would suggest that this Scripture become a cornerstone in our thinking on clothing.

HOW WE CAN SIMPLIFY OUR HOUSING AND OUR LIFESTYLE AT HOME

During the itinerant ministry walk I mentioned earlier, our group was impressed with the beauty of the countryside—the land of the Ozark and Boston mountains, the Wichita mountains, the surrounding hills of Little Rock—the beauty of nature surrounded us. It was autumn, and the leaves were turning. Then we happened upon a housing development. Clusters of tightly-packed, hundred-thousand dollar homes clashed sharply with the serenity of the natural environs. I found myself analyzing the architecture of these suburban tract homes. It seemed to illustrate the conflicting values we so often see in modern society.

The homes—built like castles complete with turrets,

large windows, and enough of a facade of brick to give a sense of stability—were patterned after colonial plantation mansions. In their time in the South, such homes would have commanded acres of surrounding land and would have been built to last for centuries. These modern structures, however, seemed overly large for the small plots of land on which they were built and appeared to come from the same architect's drawing board, like a cookie cutter design. Upon closer inspection, it was also obvious that they possessed merely the veneer of stateliness and stability. Underneath, cheap materials and quick building techniques revealed a slapdash approach to housing which draftsmen of a generation ago would have disowned as "shoddy workmanship." Expensive as they were, they attempted to appear even more so, appealing to the yuppie values so prevalent in today's suburban America.

Even more alarming, young couples mortgage themselves to the hilt just to move into one of these houses, unable to afford the furniture required to fill them up! Interestingly, when parties are thrown for their social counterparts, nice furniture is, many times, rented for the evening and then carted off the next morning, leaving echos in the partially vacant houses.

Today, it seems we want wealth and we want it now. Gone are the days when slow growth and orderly accumulation of assets built toward something of enduring value. Instead, we seem to have arrived in an era where "easy come, easy go" and "here today, gone tomorrow" values prevail. Lost is the idea that a house should first and foremost serve as shelter. Instead, today's luxury home reflects how the lifestyles of so many have become a lie—an inflated, exaggerated existence built on appearance, not content.

I am reminded of the Scripture in Isaiah 5:8 where we hear the lamentation, "Woe to you who join house to house,/who connect field with field,/Till no room remains, and you are left to dwell/alone in the midst of the land!" The following verses in this Scripture passage imply that God will sovereignly bring down this inhumane and unjust system. Such a system is headed for collapse if left unchecked. When houses are joined with other houses in cramped quarters, when floor after floor is stacked to create high-rise slabs vaulting into the sky, when apartments, condominiums, and businesses are jammed together—we create psychological havoc among people.

There is no space, there is no silence. On the contrary, there is a cacophony of noises competing for our attention, intruding into our lives. Privacy is gone, so we devise new techniques of separating ourselves from others, walling ourselves off through locks, bars, alarms, and gates. Forced together, we fear true intimacy. As noise levels rise, we chase after new meditation techniques in an attempt to find peace, solitude, and silence. But still we do not see healthy people, healthy business or a healthy society in general.

Perhaps Plato's idea of a city whose inhabitants do not number beyond a certain point is a good one. In *The Republic* he states that most people should dwell in rural areas as farmers and producers of the basic needs of society. The city is a place of specialization. Civil servants are to live in the city, along with politicians and the military—who, by the way—would measure up to a standard of selflessness and discipline. Industry would meet the genuine needs of all the people. It would not be some kind of sprawling metropolis built on artificiality and lopsided social and economic systems. I believe there is something to be said for the principles that Plato envisioned. People should be close to their needs, not far removed from them. History is replete with examples of civilizations which have become increasingly removed from their production of basic essentials, and they have fallen. Today as I have mentioned, it would seem that America is in much the same position.

I am reminded of the example of a football player. Just when a running back knows he is about to be hit, he lowers his shoulders. By standing too tall, he will certainly be knocked down by the greater force of the tackler. The closer to the ground the player is, the more stable will be his center of gravity. Likewise, civilizations must be kept close to their basic needs: food, shelter, clothing, and the other essentials of life. The more flamboyant and luxury-oriented a society becomes, the greater the crash will be when adversity befalls, as it always will.

We see this syndrome in our current approach to housing. We have produced apartments, condominiums, and suburban housing developments with increased mass-production techniques and decreased attention to quality and detail. Of course, this quick and impersonal approach to housing will have ramifications in other areas such as environmental concerns. Energy consumption is a matter of concern, for example. The very design of our houses dictates extraordinary use of fuels and resources which far exceed those of many other societies. We are continuing our cycles of waste, pollution, and inefficiency in the way we shelter ourselves.

Here at the Little Portion hermitage, we attempt to address some of these issues. We try to use advances in technology to conserve rather than to consume. For example, we use heat pumps to balance temperatures which overall is a conservation measure. As for the architecture of our living quarters, they are semi-earth shelters that take advantage of ambient earthen temperatures which cool the earth in the summer and warm it in the winter. Energy consumption is thus significantly reduced year round. Passive solar heating and skylighting futher assist in creating efficiency in our living quarters. We have even considered harnessing the wind to generate power, which is actually quite feasible in many parts of the country. Over a period of time, alternative energy sources can prove to be a great savings, particularly when communities with larger numbers of people are involved. Even single family dwellings have proven that, over a period of time, careful attention to alternative energy sources and careful selection of heating and cooling systems can result in significant conservation of resources—and funds.

The most important things which need to be converted are really not our domestic energy systems but our attitudes. Again, we find that simplicity begins within the interior realities of our lives. We must contemplate our true needs. Do we really need the stereo on as often as it is? Do we actually need three or four television sets—or even one? Must our homes be heated to 70 degrees when

65 degrees in the winter will suffice? Do we really need to turn on our air conditioners when temperatures rise to 80 degrees? Couldn't we learn to tolerate at least 80 degrees? How long should our lights be on? These and related questions must be considered to ferret out our wants from our needs. We need to rethink these issues and then make any necessary modifications to simplify the way we live in our homes.

Sometimes we find that our cultural hang-ups impede us from models of living which are highly efficient. Consider, for example, the dry toilet system we have begun using in our community. As Westerners, we're culturally tied to the idea of neatly disposing of human wastes through flush-toilet systems. In doing so, we create problems. Each flush drains away three to five gallons of precious, fresh water—rendering it virtually useless for anything, other than transporting our excretions to collection points where other problems are created, such as how exactly to deal with millions of gallons of sewage. Not only are dry toilet systems far less expensive to operate, they can actually recycle wastes for use in composting, fertilizing, and methane gas production which can be used to fuel gas stoves. Unfortunately, it will take a minor cultural revolution to bring this kind of efficiency into any kind of widespread use in our society.

It has been interesting for me to study historical expressions of Christian lifestyles from the early church in Jerusalem, through the itinerant ministries of the apostles, European and Middle Eastern monastic developments, and Franciscan approaches to community. Here, at the Little Portion hermitage we have attempted to adapt Franciscan lifestyle ideals to our own modern setting and

circumstances. We have attempted to build a semi-ere-
mitical pattern into a basic Franciscan approach to
community. Thus, we have clustered our hermitages
around a common chapel and a common building. In the
common building—a simple metal structure—we have a
kitchen, a dining area, a craft room, recreation space, a
small library, and a cluster of small offices. Each hermitage
is decorated very simply and has a bed, a small desk, and a
chair. We create some private prayer space for individuals
in their domiciles, and basic water and sanitary conditions are met. While some might consider our living
spaces rather spartan, we actually allow for enough open
space, light, and ventilation to ensure psychological and
physical health.

We also attempt to address individual needs. For that
reason, you will find structures which are further sepa-
rated from the main community for those with a commitment to a more solitary kind of spirituality. Likewise,
there are postulants and novices who may live in different
contexts, depending upon their commitment to the community, their ultimate intentions, and their personal
needs. There are also families living in our communities
who have needs beyond those of the celibate brother and
sister. Then there are individual ministries which must be
considered: musicians need practicing space and sound
insulation for recording. A dancer may need special consideration when it comes to workouts and performing.
Obviously, uniformity is not our goal or our ethic. Rather,
simplicity and appropriate diversity work together in
a communal context for the good of all and for the glory
of God.

If the serious Christian is willing to incorporate values based on gospel poverty into these primary areas of life—food, clothing, and shelter—great steps will be taken forward in simplifying his or her life. Of course, there are many areas related to these three categories which have not been treated. There are many other concerns that are beyond the scope of this book. However, the same attitudes which must be developed in the three areas mentioned express the attitudes and convictions required to address other areas in living a simple life.

Whatever the issue or area, we must keep distinguishing between two basic things: our wants and our needs. Individuals will arrive at somewhat different conclusions as they begin to address these issues. Spiritual maturity will vary. Human needs will be different. Professional considerations will change, and various ministries will need to be addressed differently. Diversity is okay! It is only important that an honest attempt be made to consider all our options. Then we can begin to choose a simpler, more meaningful life.

Practical Pointers on How to Simplify Your Life on Planet Earth

1) What happens when a society such as ours becomes oriented to wants rather than needs? Name some effects of this imbalance.

2) What are the three basic needs for human existence according to Scripture? How are you faring in meeting these basic needs for yourself and your family? Have these needs become wants?

3) Consider each of the three basic needs for human existence. Highlight one practical way you can simplify your life in meeting each of the three basic needs.

4) Take some time for prayer and counsel with Christians you trust about these three areas. Then decide to make a definite change in one of the three areas. Carry through with your decision in a spirit of humility, in obedience to God, and in daily prayer.

SEVEN

Living in Community, Serving the Poor, and Taking Political Action

IN THIS BOOK, I HAVEN'T GLOSSED OVER the hard fact that seeking simplicity in our lives can be difficult, sometimes frightening, and downright sacrificial. Let's face it, life is a struggle. And certainly, if we attempt to daily bear our crosses and follow Christ, our faith pilgrimage will also be a struggle, though hopefully a joyful one. When we attempt to radically follow Christ on our own, the challenge becomes even more substantial—that's why we need other brothers and sisters to assist us and provide support. This is the value of community life.

It is together that our load is lightened and it is together, in the body of Christ, that we are redeemed as a people. It is out of groups, often specific organizations, that programs emerge which assist us in our Christian walk, including our goal of simple living. Programs can provide a kind of outline to follow or—if you will—a skeletal framework on which to "flesh out" our Christian lives as we build toward our objectives. Often, without a program or a plan, we wander aimlessly in our pilgrimage or repeatedly fail. That's why structure can be helpful.

There are many concepts and strategies we might consider in developing or following an effective program for simplicity. But instead of discussing programmatic theories, I want to present three concrete models of programs that hold promise. One of them is the structure of our own community, the Brothers and Sisters of Charity. Another is the relief and development ministry we support, Franciscan Mercy Corps, which is a division of Mercy Corps International. Finally, because we believe political action must be expressed in appropriate ways, we will consider an organization which is still under formation called the Christian Political Option. These three programs are only meant to serve as examples of ways Christians are called to live out gospel simplicity together.

LIVING A COMMITTED COMMUNITY LIFE: THE BROTHERS AND SISTERS OF CHARITY

The Brothers and Sisters of Charity are our community members who either live here at the Little Portion hermitage or in their own homes united by one Scripture rule, constitution, and general leadership. As an integrated community we include a single, celibate, and married monastic expression, as well as a domestic expression for those who live in their own homes. Each group has its own particular statutes and leadership. As such, we are a microcosm of the whole church.

Let us, however, consider here the domestic expression of the "Little Brothers and Sisters of Charity." How do they express the ideals of a monastic community that lives intentional community life in a hermitage? These members simply apply the spirituality of our rule and constitution to their own particular circumstances, in their homes, or wherever they may be, according to their own particular state in life and vocation. To us, they are full community members. However, they do not necessarily live in intentional community life.

There are seven covenant promises which all members of our community profess:

1. We live a life of gospel poverty so that others might know the wealth of the kingdom of God.

2. We are committed to a life of chastity, both marital and celibate, so that others might know the love of our divine Lover, Jesus Christ.

3. We commit ourselves to a life of obedience so that others might know the directed freedom of the truth and the love in God in their own lives.

4. We are committed to substantial solitude so that others might know the divine companionship of Jesus.

5. We live lives of substantial silence so that others might hear the living Word of God incarnate in their lives.

6. We live a life of penance or conversion so that others may be motivated to turn back to God, receiving his forgiveness and experiencing rebirth.

7. We are committed to a life of prayer so that others might know the divine action of God in their own lives.

Essentially, these are seven covenants which each member takes. Of course, we live them out in somewhat different ways, depending upon the different states of life in which we find ourselves. The celibate brothers and sisters live out the vows of poverty, chastity, and obedience in more intense ways—possessing nothing, vowing celibate chastity, and committing to very specific levels of obedience to the church, to community guidelines, and in their private lives.

This is a more strict, more focused expression of poverty, chastity, and obedience. However, I believe that all are called to some level of gospel poverty and obedience. Obviously, we cannot and do not expect those outside our immediate community to live out vows or covenant promises which are unrealistic for their state of life. This is particularly true in view of the fact that we believe in the primacy of the family. And among families needs and situations differ widely. Also we are careful not to take inappropriate authority over the domestic affairs of families associated with our community. We feel that, as in any family, there are private affairs that are rightly reserved for the family's jurisdiction alone.

We do not expect everyone to spend more than half their day in solitude and silence, but we do urge indi-

vidual members to take time daily for some form of meditation, contemplation, or charismatic prayer. Time alone
with God is very important in maintaining and deepening
our spiritual commitment. We promote all forms of prayer
including contemplative, spontaneous, and liturgical
forms. Also certain ascetical practices or disciplines, such
as fasting, are encouraged as each person or family deems
appropriate.

In our extended community of the Little Brothers and
Sisters of Charity, there are various elements which have
been integrated into our life which I would like to discuss.
First, there is an integration between the contemplative
and the charismatic. We are an overtly charismatic community, open to the free working of the charismatic gifts.
However, we are very much aware of the need for the
contemplative life. There is also integration between solitude and community. Time alone with God is balanced
against the responsibilities and blessings of communal
life, which should also be true of the Christian family.

Another point of balance in the community is contemplation and apostolic action. Of course, we encourage
every family and every local intentional community to
have daily, weekly, and monthly times of prayer together.
Occasions for group or solitary prayer are extremely
important, but so is involvement in various apostolic
ministries. These may be undertaken individually or as
a group.

Finally, we are a Catholic-based, ecumenical community, so there is an integration of many Christian
traditions, while respecting the uniqueness and integrity
of each. Of course, as a Catholic-based community, we

treasure and protect orthodox doctrine and have a rich sacramental life. We are a uniquely Catholic community which is open to other expressions of Christian faith. Any Christian able to profess either the Apostle's Creed or the Nicene Creed as statements of orthodoxy would easily fit into the Brothers and Sisters of Charity. We are also open to drawing from the wisdom and beauty of other faith expressions outside of Christianity, but this is done with discretion and caution.

We feel God has given us some important, prophetic guidance about the structure of this community. We felt the need to "die to Franciscanism." This simply means that what we are doing is different and bigger than a purely Franciscan expression of community. This isn't to say that it is better. Rather, we are building on the entire monastic and religious tradition of the past, focusing heavily on going back to the Gospels themselves as the primary inspiration for our communities. Also because we are attempting something which is quite new, we don't want to put new wine into old wineskins. This is another reason we feel that we do not fit any pre-existing category of canon law or Franciscan structure. It would seem God is giving us something special for our own time—in the same way that he worked through St. Francis, St. Benedict, St. Basil, and others who were led by God in a special way during their own times. As such, we see Franciscanism as our mother, but having been birthed, we constitute an entity that is unique and new.

In our community, we profess covenant promises rather than vows. Classically, the Evangelical Counsels of poverty, chastity, and obedience were vowed in community in very legal and strict ways. But as community has developed historically the emphasis and duration of vows has varied. We feel that covenant promises are an expression of our own era—that covenant community is being raised up by the Spirit of God today. As such, our covenants include everything that has come before. Yet they also include something which is fresh and different.

The covenant promises mean that while a commitment is made, the commitments are temporary yet renewable. Therefore, our expectation is not that the covenant promise will necessarily be a permanent one. Rather, a commitment is made with the possibility of it becoming permanent at some future time. This allows a broader representation of Christians to enter into meaningful commitments, while solemn, lifelong vows are only entered into by a few. In this way, guilt and failure are avoided in favor of periodic promises which are made as God leads, always leaving room for personal choice and new direction. It is our experience that God wishes to lead people into religious life for temporary periods of time. They are renewed and gain a greater depth of spirituality. Then they can return to the secular world to live out their faith in a more powerful way.

It should be stressed that while there is freedom, the covenant promises are also real commitments which we feel are urgent in a world experiencing fractured families, dissolving businesses, crumbling communities, and other relationships in crisis. The covenant promise brings stability into a Christian community and builds committed relationships.

Another new dimension of our community is that

varied expressions of lifestyle are possible: We include single, celibate, and married members in our monastic expression, with singles and marrieds in our domestic expression. As such we are a microcosm of the whole church. We consider this to be one community with varying, particular expressions. Obviously, this is different from a traditional approach to religious community.

As one community—a community without borders you might say—we all have the same rule. We have assembled this rule based entirely on Scriptures. We call it the *Scripture Rule*. It is made up of some 150 Scriptures with no elaboration. Also we have one general constitution for the entire community which outlines general principles of lifestyle. However, each individual expression of our community has its own developing set of statutes which describe particular lifestyle expectations and norms.

There are also general government and particular government. For example, the brothers have their own leadership which is distinct from the leadership of the sisters. Of course, the sisters have their own leadership as well. Singles and families in our community have their own leaders. This also holds true of community members throughout the country who have their own leadership council. As the community develops, there will undoubtedly be more regional and local leadership considerations. These all exist under the leadership of one general council which is guided by one general rule and one general constitution. The general council consists at this point of leaders from among the celibate brothers, the celibate sisters, the singles, and families at the Little Portion hermitage as well as the council of the Little Brothers and Sisters of Charity.

This is a radical break with the past. We feel it speaks to the present need to overcome the social fragmentation and class system which can easily develop not only in the world but in expressions of monastic and religious communities. We are one community! We are all Brothers and Sisters of Charity. However, there are different particular expressions of how we live out that communal spirituality. One is not better than the other—they are simply different.

Another prophetic word we discerned was that we were to "build community by not building community." We have tried to put aside all unnecessary preconceived notions of how to build religious community. This means that the real building of community must be God's work, not ours. God is bringing together all kinds of different people into a new communal expression of faith. He is not simply bringing people to join our way of life at the Little Portion hermitage—he is calling Christians from all over the world, right where they are, to live simple lives based on gospel poverty and to move toward community in a particular way. In this way, God is surprising us with outpourings of his Spirit. We are seeing deep spiritual experiences of tongues, tears, raptures, ecstasies, and some of the very signs and wonders which accompanied so many of the saints throughout history. At the same time, God is also instilling within us a great love for liturgy and contemplation. God is blessing us with something old and something new as tradition is empowered in the Spirit to form a new model.

While I see evidence of exciting new releases of the Holy Spirit, we have no illusions about the real challenges and sacrifices which confront us. It's sometimes easy to fall into a feel-good mentality—that warm spiritual glow of God's presence. But more is required. Along with the empowerment comes sacrifice and the ongoing challenge of making real community work. Within community, we continue to strive for new levels and expressions of simplicity of lifestyle. We believe that the Brothers and Sisters of Charity and the Little Brothers and Sisters of Charity represent a new expression of community which will help pave the way toward the future. It is a new wineskin, even now continuing to expand as God leads through his Spirit and our experience of Christian Community.

USING OUR RESOURCES TO SERVE THE POOR: FRANCISCAN MERCY CORPS

Mercy Corps International is an ecumenical, Christian relief and development organization working with the poorest of the poor around the world. I have found Mercy Corps to be a highly efficient organization in its international programs and handling of funds. A number of years ago when I felt led of God to do concerts and raise funds for famine victims in Africa, I joined forces with Mercy Corps International and now serve as honorary chairman. Out of this relationship grew Franciscan Mercy Corps, a program of Mercy Corps International and the relief and development arm of the community movement

I mentioned above. It is the means by which the Brothers and Sisters of Charity can reach out, minister to the needs of the poor, and belong to an organization rather than simply giving to an organization.

Franciscan Mercy Corps is an ecumenical group of people who gather locally to support one another through prayer, study, and service. We take seriously the gospel mandate to respond to the needs of both our domestic and foreign poor. This is done primarily through Franciscan inspiration because of the tremendous example of St. Francis, and because Franciscan expressions of Christian faith are largely ecumenical.

Franciscan Mercy Corps involves cell groups of individuals who meet together at least monthly. We ask that people specifically pray about the problem of global poverty as well as peace and social justice issues. As is the case with the Little Brothers and Sisters of Charity, we emphasize a highly integrated approach to prayer, involving liturgical, charismatic, and contemplative approaches. We also encourage members to become involved with the sacraments as they are understood and ministered in their own particular churches.

Because we believe that it is important to study relevant social issues within Franciscan Mercy Corps (FMC) cell groups, we urge serious reading of the Scriptures (especially the Gospels), Franciscan sources, and pertinent church documents—such as Vatican II documents which we find to be ecumenically applicable to any Christian. Also important are such documents as Pope John Paul II's encyclical *On Social Concern*. Documents from other Christian faiths have made significant contributions as well, such as *In Defense of Creation* by the Methodists. Insofar as church documents are ecumenically appropriate, we encourage the cell groups to use them.

Individual FMC members and cell groups are requested to serve the poor in some way. We encourage them to serve in their own geographical areas and to work within existing organizations such as the St. Vincent De Paul Society, the Meals on Wheels program, soup kitchen service, food bank projects, and prison ministries. As a practical consideration, we urge cell groups not to "reinvent the wheel" by founding a new ministry, but rather to collaborate with other ministries and institutions that are open to partnerships.

As members learn to simplify their own lives, financial and material resources are freed to serve the poor, whether through local efforts or through Mercy Corps International's well-established relief and development programs in other parts of the world. Monies have even been raised to send FMC volunteers to work overseas for periods of time. I should point out that any individual volunteer must have certain qualifications, training, and testing before overseas assignments are made.

Mercy Corps International, through its publications and conferences, attempts to educate FMC members and other American Christians on how the poor may be most efficiently helped. For this reason Mercy Corps is committed to the philosophy of development—a self-help approach which enables people to take responsibility for their own well-being, allowing them self-determination, and ultimately enabling them to reach out to help others instead of simply receiving help themselves. Obviously,.

there are times when relief is needed in such situations as famine disasters and catastrophic events such as earthquakes or wars. In this case, relief may be defined as whatever assistance is needed to sustain life at a normal level. Development, on the other hand, allows people to choose for themselves the path which will better their lives with technical input from Mercy Corps experts.

A most important program which Mercy Corps International incorporates into its global ministry is faith development. We believe that it is extremely important to minister to the whole person in an integrated way so that all needs are met: physical, mental, emotional, and spiritual.

I have traveled with Mercy Corps chairman Dan O'Neill, and its president Ells Culver, to visit development projects in such areas as the Philippines and Honduras. We have also taken trips to investigate problems with Christian Palestinian refugees in the Middle East. I am convinced that as American Christians share more generously out of their substance by giving sacrificially, an enormous impact can be made in alleviating the plight of the poor. And we know that in ministering to the world's poor, we are actually ministering to Jesus himself as the mystery of the incarnation confronts us all around the world. As Mother Teresa says, in the poorest of the poor we encounter the distressing disguise of Christ.

Mercy Corps International and Franciscan Mercy Corps represent real opportunities for putting simplicity into practice, for appropriately sharing with the Third World poor, for touching needs in our own areas, and for continuing our own faith pilgrimage. For further information you may write: Mercy Corps, Portland, Oregon 97201.

TAKING POLITICAL ACTION:
THE CHRISTIAN POLITICAL OPTION

"Let them individually and collectively be in the forefront in promoting justice by the testimony of their human lives and their courageous initiatives, especially in the fields of public life that they should make definite choices in harmony with their faith." This statement comes from the *Secular Franciscan Rule*. The new constitutions of the Order of Friars Minor speak more specifically about taking appropriate political action. There are also many official church statements and documents which urge us to seriously consider our roles and responsibilities as citizens. In the Vatican II document, *The Church in the Modern World*, we read:

It is in full accord with human nature that juridical-political structures should, with even better success and without any discrimination, afford all their citizens the chance to participate freely and actively in establishing the constitutional bases of political community governing the state, determining the scope and purpose of various institutions and choosing their leaders. Hence, let all citizens be mindful of their simultaneous right and duty to freely vote in the interest of advancing the common good. The church regards as worthy of praise and consideration, the work of those who, as a service to others, dedicate themselves to the welfare of the state and undertake the burdens of this task. (No. 75)

Here the church states that we have not only the right but the duty to become involved in the political situation in which we find ourselves. Whether we like it or not, political parties and other such structures are a reality which must be faced by Christians. They affect our lives and the lives of all citizens not only in our nation, but around the world in many ways. This responsibility becomes a given for us, whether voting locally to build a new school in our community or voting nationally on a matter which will have immense foreign policy consequences on an international level.

I would emphasize at this point that the Brothers and Sisters of Charity, Mercy Corps International, and Franciscan Mercy Corps do not see politics as a primary mission, but as an overflow from our primary conversion to Christ, life in community, and concern for the world's poor. We see a responsibility which must be assumed if we are to be Christians of conscience, obedient to the directives of the church, and to the call of the gospel. We are not called to be political radicals—we are called to be radical Christians. In fulfilling this call, we must be renewed before we can renew others. We must experience the peace of Christ before we can speak about real peace in the world. We must be justified by the grace of God before we can bring justice into the world.

There are, for example, many liberation movements around the world which claim to be Christian but use Marxist analysis and other ideological dialectics in addressing the problem of unjust social structures. While it may be good to overthrow a despotic dictatorship, we must be careful that we do not replace one unjust system with another—a warning that the pope has given in addressing the problem of liberation theology, particularly in Latin American countries. Our first liberation must be from sin and death. Our first liberation must be in Christ. It is from this foundation that we may go forth, as servants, attempting to renew the temporal order by exercising our political rights and duties.

There are three pivotal issues facing us today, among many others, which I feel must be addressed through appropriate political action. The first is the issue of abortion. In America alone forty-five hundred abortions are performed every day, nearly ten thousand every two days. While we should be concerned with all human life issues, from conception to the grave, abortion is, as Cardinal Bernard Law has stated, ". . . the primordial darkness of our time. This is the cloud that shrouds the conscience of our world. Having made our peace with the death of the most innocent among us, it is small wonder that we are so ineffective when dealing with hunger, injustice, and the threat of nuclear war."

If we fail to save the most innocent among us, how can we deal effectively with issues of war, hunger, injustice? What we face in today's world is an international holocaust. From the Soviet Union to the United States, from India to Israel, abortions are committed at an unprecedented pace, wiping out the innocent lives of millions. Most of us have seen the pictures. We have all heard the arguments. Books have been written and demonstrations abound. This dreadful sin, however, continues every day, an unseen massacre of unspeakable proportions which continues with the legal blessing of our Supreme Court.

Here is a moral issue. Yet it is also a political issue requiring our thoughtful, forceful response. We bear a responsibility to the unborn, whether through our vote or through our demonstration of concern.

Another pressing issue is the nuclear arms race. In spite of superpower talks and the dismantling of some nuclear weapons, enough nuclear firepower exists to destroy the earth and its inhabitants many times over. We have created scientific weapons of massive—and indiscriminate—destruction. The arms race has gone beyond the legitimate needs of defense. In order to maintain our comfortable American lifestyles, we are willing to hold a gun at the head of the world. The Catholic church and other church bodies have been unhesitating in condemning even the threat of nuclear war. As Christians with political responsibilities, we must address these issues through our votes and through the influence we wield as taxpaying citizens.

Another primary concern we all face is the plight of the global poor. Billions go to bed hungry every night. Forty thousand a day, by one United Nations estimate, die of malnutrition and related diseases. Women and children are affected the most. It is imperative that American citizens consider their role in addressing the question of urgent, international human need. It is certainly no secret to those who have studied social justice issues that American foreign policy has, in fact, helped to subjugate peoples in some cases.Through misguided economic policies and military pressures even more oppression, poverty, and death has resulted in certain Latin American countries and elsewhere.

How do we address these issues as American Christians? It would seem that we are caught on the horns of a great dilemma. When one examines the party platforms of the Democrats and Republicans, neither fulfills the consistent life ethic we would wish to see uplifted. While Democrats, for example, are more progressive in certain social issues regarding the poor, they are unabashedly committed to promoting a so-called pro-choice policy on abortion. The Republicans, who are predominantly pro-life, are nevertheless historically less sensitive to the needs of the poor and more committed to the arms build-up "peace through strength" policy. Where are we to turn?

The pope himself has spoken eloquently about the excesses of the left and the right, the unacceptability of Marxism and unbridled capitalism. As he says in his encyclical *On Social Concern,* "The Church's social doctrine adopts a critical attitude towards liberal capitalism and Marxist collectivism" (No. 21). However, the social doctrine of the church is not the primary issue. The pope cautions, "The teaching and spreading of her social doctrine are part of the Church's evangelizing mission:... The condemnation of evils and injustices is also part of that ministry of evangelization in the social field, which is an aspect of the Church's prophetic role. But it should be made clear that proclamation is more important than condemnation, and the later cannot ignore the former which gives it its true solidarity and higher motivation."

Politically and socially the pope is saying this: Jesus, and Jesus alone, must remain the pivot point of all our ideological and political involvements. If we ever remove Jesus from that central focus and place politics or a particular governmental system there instead, we have committed the sin of idolatry. Many Christian Marxist movements have taken Marxism and placed it at the center, while using Jesus' own words to justify their particular political involvement. The same can be said about many of the new Christian Right conservatives of capitalism. This, too, is the sin of idolatry. All of us, whether capitalists, Marxists, or somewhere in between, must have Jesus at the very center of our personal life. From this foundation, we will be able to take appropriate social and political action within our modern world.

I would like to use as examples of appropriate political involvement Cardinal Jaime Sin of the Philippines and our Christian Palestinian brothers and sisters. Recently, there was a peaceful revolution in the Philippines that overthrew a horribly oppressive government under the Marcos regime, where the rich grew richer and the poor got poorer. It had reached an intolerable level in 1986.

There were no existing structures for change which the people of the Philippines could use, except for the church. Key leaders from among the people went to Cardinal Sin begging him to get involved, saying that there would be a revolution and it would be soon. They stressed that if he did not get involved the revolution would end in chaos and widespread, massive bloodshed.

Cardinal Jaime Sin used religious radio broadcasts in the Philippines to get out his message. He called the people to rise up in revolution, a revolution not of violence and bloodshed, but a revolution of peace. He told them to pray.

During this peaceful revolution, the Marcos regime responded with guns and tanks and bombs. However,

God worked miracle after miracle. He turned back fighter pilots from strafing the crowds with bullets by speaking to them in the depths of their hearts about the sin of taking such action against innocent people. He caused tank gunners to see deceased relatives among the crowds, and they could not in good conscience fire upon the people. The people passed out flowers and crucifixes and rosaries to military personnel and won them over through love and prayer.

I am not saying that this revolution was ideal, nor was it without problems. We all know that the Philippines have gone through immense struggles and growing pains as the country has come out of this miraculous rebirth into the normal growth pangs of a struggling, developing nation. But there was a central focus on the gospel of Jesus Christ and his way of peace which overflowed into the political arena. It brought forth a miraculous and peaceful revolution, one of the few that has occurred in all of human history. We cannot claim such a revolution in the United States. Though we were founded on religious principles, much blood was shed which tainted the very soil we were trying to claim during the American Revolutionary War. The Philippines revolution centered more firmly on Jesus, and much less bloodshed was involved.

It is interesting to note that when Dan O'Neill, Ells Culver, and I visited with Cardinal Jaime Sin in our recent visit to the Philippines, this so-called political revolutionary for Christ spoke of nothing but Jesus and his humble mother, Mary. Not once did he bring up the topic of politics or social concern, or even economics as an emphasis. Even though we were there as a relief and development agency, the Cardinal repeatedly brought the conversation back to his primary concern, the gospel of Jesus Christ.

We walked away from that encounter both confused and edified. We had come as a relief and development agency, much concerned for the social, economic, and even the political plight we found among the poorest of the poor in the areas in which we worked in the Philippines. Yet the cardinal saw Jesus, and Jesus alone, along with his mother, as the model through which we would be able to succeed.

The same could be said of our recent visit to the Middle East to investigate the plight of our Palestinian Christian brothers and sisters under Israeli occupation. There, too, we found a witness of the gospel in a highly politicized and oppressive situation.

We met devout Christians who were actively involved in the struggle for Palestinian autonomy and an end to human rights abuses. They were not violent revolutionaries but brothers and sisters of good will, serving in very trying circumstances and using non-violent means to try to bring about change. For instance, we visited with Christian Palestinian leaders and they did not hesitate to preach the gospel of Jesus, even in the presence of their Moslem Palestinian friends. I will never forget one Anglican bishop standing up to enthusiastically preach the love and truth of Jesus Christ in the midst of a gathering of Christian and Moslem Palestinian leaders. Like Cardinal Jaime Sin, he is a man who seems to have his priorities straight: first, Jesus; then, people of all faiths; and, finally, political involvement when it is appropriate.

What, then, can we of the West do about pressing social, economic, and political problems? As I thought and prayed on these many issues with like-minded Christian leaders, we began to contemplate an alternative—an option. We called it the Christian Political Option. Idealistic as it might seem, it would provide Christians who subscribe to a similar consistent life ethic with the opportunity to express themselves through a political voice on a national level. It is an idea whose time may well have arrived. There is still much thought and organization which must be done. I frankly admit that I don't know where this option is leading. There are some who sincerely believe that a third political expression, beyond the Democratic and Republican parties, could result in political influence. Perhaps there are even the makings of another political party in the future. Obviously, this would be a vast undertaking, but one which should not be discarded out of hand.

This could involve a political and social evolution of sorts as we Christians respond to the critical issues of our age. Such a response does have precedence when we study the pages of Western history. We know, for instance, that in speaking of ancient Western civilization, political and social progress came as warring primitive tribes gave way to powerful kingdoms and empires. In fact, at the height of ancient Greece's glory, the philosopher Plato began to treat the very concept of civilization in his famous work, *The Republic*.

Upon this Greek understanding of civilization, the Romans built a colossal empire that spanned the Mediterranean and established an unprecedented period of peace and prosperity. It was under the stability and order of Roman rule that Christianity took root and eventually overthrew paganism in the West.

Other reknowned kingdoms and empires followed in Christian Europe: among them the empire of Charlemagne, the Spanish empire of the sixteenth century, and eventually the British empire in the nineteenth and twentieth centuries. While these kingdoms and empires clearly had their faults, they did bring Christian ideals and gospel principles to bear on pressing social and political problems.

We know that America's founding fathers took the process a step farther, framing the political and social ideals of personal freedom and individual rights as the law of the land in the United States Constitution. In turn, America's successful experiment with democracy has inspired peoples in other lands to set up democratic governments, based on these same ideals and rights. And such notions of personal freedom and the dignity of the human person are, in large part, rooted in the West's Christian heritage.

With our critical world situation today, surely the question must be asked: Perhaps it is time for another major step in our political and social evolution, informed by Christian principles? After all, what we see is unparalleled in the annals of human history. Grave economic inequities exist between the First and Third Worlds. Abortion on demand is the status quo in nearly all of our Western democracies. We are rapidly destroying our environment and virtually holding the world hostage with our nuclear arsenals of mass destruction.

While the church herself does not emphasize or center on any of these concerns as her primary mission, we cannot help but recognize this option. Our involvement can and should come as an overflow from our more primary mission of evangelization to the gospel of Jesus Christ and living simply for him.

Perhaps it is adherence to the consistent life ethic that could unify all peoples Catholic, Protestant, Orthodox, and concerned non-Christians in a new political consensus. If we could grasp together the true value of all human life and how it should be protected, then all of the major world issues of abject poverty in the Third World, abortion on demand, nuclear arms, and even destruction of the environment might come into clearer focus. This consistent life ethic, which is central to Catholic teaching, could prove to be a gift to all of humankind, regardless of political and social structures.

These, then, are the programs for simplicity that we suggest: one, on the level of Christian community, exemplified in the Brothers and Sisters of Charity; the second, on the level of relief and development, modeled by Franciscan Mercy Corps; and the third, on the level of political action, modeled by the Christian Political Option. Of course, there are many other examples of each level of involvement.

CONCLUSION

Where do all of these reflections on simple living lead us? In this book, we have attempted to show that simple living is *not* simplistic living. It involves internal choices and external actions. It is a pruning back, a dying with Jesus on the cross to internal attitudes and unnecessary external comforts and things. But these changes don't just bring death, they bring resurrection life. Pruning the tree doesn't kill it, it causes it to be more fruitful. This pruning process occurs on the level of humility, obedience, prayer, self-discipline, our approach to possessions and materialism, and our care for the environment. Ultimately, it must come out of the communities we are a part of, the works of mercy we perform or support, and the various political parties or forces for change that we are involved in. All of these dimensions are transformed if we choose to simplify our life.

This simplicity ranges all the way from our thoughts to our emotions, from our words to our actions; it effects every aspect of our life. We are not advocating a simplistic approach which merely mimics certain externals of gospel poverty or simplicity; we are advocating a simplicity which brings a true vibrancy and richness to our lives and to the life of all the world. It is a simplicity that first embraces the poverty of Jesus Christ to the glory of God as a shining witness to the world.

Practical Pointers on Living in Community, Serving the Poor, and Taking Political Action

1) How are each of the three models that have been presented expressions of the call to live a corporate Christian life and to serve others?

2) All Christians are called to live out some expression of Christian community whether in a parish, a religious community, a covenant community, or in some other context. Such expressions of community should involve a committed Christian life, where brothers and sisters in Christ support each other in loving and

serving God. Do you live in committed Christian community? If so, explain. If not, why?

3) Giving alms and serving those in need are part of the basic gospel call. Such acts are called the corporal works of mercy. Giving to a Christian relief and development agency is one expression of the corporal works of mercy. Are you responding to this call in your Christian life? If so, how? If not, why?

4) Are you involved or have you ever considered getting involved in politics? Should a Christian ever be involved in politics? If so, what kind of political involvement might be right for you? If not, why?

5) Take some time for prayer and seek the counsel of Christians you trust in discerning whether God wants you to move ahead in one of these three areas. Once you've made a decision, carry through in a spirit of humility, in obedience to God, and in daily prayer.

Other Books of Interest from Servant Publications

Reflections on the Gospels
Volume One
by John Michael Talbot

Daily meditations on various readings from the gospels that reveal much of what motivated John Michael Talbot to abandon all in order to follow Christ and live a simple life, marked by obedience, poverty, and humility. Containing approximately four months of daily meditations, *Reflections on the Gospels, Volume One* speaks of our need to have faith, to be honest about our failings, and to put everything we have in the hands of Christ. *$6.95*

Reflections on the Gospels
Volume Two
by John Michael Talbot

This companion edition to Volume One contains approximately four additional months of daily meditations on various readings from the gospels. Talbot continues to call all Christians to live radically for Christ. His concise, to-the-point reflections will challenge Christians to examine the depth and quality of their response to that gospel. *$6.95*

Available at your Christian bookstore or from:
**Servant Publications • Dept. 209 • P.O. Box 7455
Ann Arbor, Michigan 48107**
Please include payment plus $1.25 per book
for postage and handling.
*Send for our FREE catalog of Christian
books, music, and cassettes.*